HARNESS the POWER
of REFLECTION

Continuous School Improvement
From the Front Office to the Classroom

RON NASH

CORWIN

A SAGE Company

CORWIN
A SAGE Company

FOR INFORMATION:

Corwin
A SAGE Company
2455 Teller Road
Thousand Oaks, California 91320
(800) 233-9936
Fax: (800) 417-2466
www.corwin.com

SAGE Ltd.
1 Oliver's Yard
55 City Road
London EC1Y 1SP
United Kingdom

SAGE India Pvt. Ltd.
B 1/I 1 Mohan Cooperative Industrial Area
Mathura Road, New Delhi 110 044
India

SAGE Asia-Pacific Pte. Ltd.
33 Pekin Street #02-01
Far East Square
Singapore 048763

Acquisitions Editor: Hudson Perigo
Associate Editor: Allison Scott
Editorial Assistant: Lisa Whitney
Production Editor: Veronica Stapleton
Copy Editor: Matthew Sullivan
Typesetter: C&M Digitals (P) Ltd.
Proofreader: Dennis W. Webb
Indexer: Rick Hurd
Cover Designer: Karine Hovsepian
Permissions Editor: Adele Hutchinson

Printed in the United States of America

Library of Congress Cataloging-in-Publication Data

Nash, Ron J.

Harness the power of reflection : continuous school improvement from the front office to the classroom / Ron Nash.

p. cm.
Includes bibliographical references and index.

ISBN 978-1-4129-9267-1 (pbk.)

1. School improvement programs—United States. I. Title.

LB2822.82.N34 2011 371.2′07—dc22 2010049311

This book is printed on acid-free paper.

11 12 13 14 15 10 9 8 7 6 5 4 3 2 1

Contents

Preface

In 2000, I attended the National Staff Development Conference in Dallas and took that occasion to visit the headquarters and manufacturing facility of Texas Nameplate, Inc., a 1998 Small Business Baldrige National Quality Award winner. Dale Crownover, Texas Nameplate's president and CEO, took the time to give me an extended tour of the facility—home to just under 100 employees. He and his management team took me to lunch, and we discussed the benefits that accrue to everyone in an organization that is committed to continuous improvement.

What impressed me most about the visit is that although I came from a *school district* 1,400 miles away, and although what I was touring was a company that makes metal nameplates, during my three-hour visit *we spoke a common language*. We spoke of processes, systems, customer service, feedback, results, and many other things that every organization has in common. They enjoyed having me there, and I had much to learn from this small business that had made such a large impact in the world of identification nameplates.

Texas Nameplate won the Baldrige Award again in 2004. As of this writing, Crownover and his company are pursuing this prestigious national award yet again, but he will be the first to say that it is not about the award; *it is about the journey*. It is about the *quest* for improvement. It is all about the commitment of everyone in the organization as they strive toward a common goal. The continuous-improvement journey is one that never ends; this is why I despair when I see schools celebrate achieving state accreditation, literally raise the inevitable flag, *and then relax*. In the course of a true continuous-improvement journey, *the tests will take care of themselves—* but they are not the goal. In the best classrooms with the most successful teachers and students, it is about the journey; it is about refusing to believe that where we are *now* is anywhere near good enough. It is about preparing students for their future.

Organizations are composed of people, and it is ultimately the people of any organization who will be responsible for its success or failure. Show me a fractious school staff and I will show you a fractious student body. Show me a school with dynamic leadership and a commitment to service and improvement, and I will show you a student body that not only thrives but—for the most part—also loves coming to school every day. Show me a school with an administration unwilling or unable to support staff, and I will show you low morale and a high absentee rate.

What impresses me about Dale Crownover and Texas Nameplate is that they never let up; they are in a constant state of "How can we make who and what we are better" and "How can we improve processes in a way that will benefit not only our customers but also those with whom we work." For Texas Nameplate, it is a matter of commitment, action, and persistence in the face of difficulties.

What can be said of this great company can be said of equally great schools and districts committed to continuous improvement and results. This book is intended to help schools in their own pursuit of purposeful progress and concrete results. In eight chapters, we'll lay the groundwork for those willing to take an honest look at where they are, and then put in place a set of processes that will get them where they want to go. We'll see how a true commitment to improvement can positively affect morale, performance, and the way parents and students view what is going on in the schoolhouse.

Beyond what can be done at the district or building level, individual teachers, or teachers working in small groups or grade-level teams, can accomplish much. There is no need for individual teachers to wait until "the powers that be" decree that improvement is now job one. Individual teachers concerned about improvement for its own sake *are* the powers that be in their own classrooms. Teachers who want to begin their own continuous-improvement journey need not wait for a signal or a starter pistol in order to hit the ground running. An elementary teacher need only look into the faces of her 30 fifth graders to know that putting in place a system for continuous improvement can't wait for direction from above, if none is forthcoming. She and her students have a vested interest in starting down the continuous-improvement highway beginning now. *Her* progress is *their* progress, and their progress depends to a large extent on her determination to get better at what *she* does every single day.

Opportunities for continuous improvement spill out from the classrooms and into the buildings and grounds that make up the campus. There are schoolwide systems in need of processes, and processes in need of improvement. If the hallways are noisy and chaotic places, it does not have to be that way. If visitors are met with indifference at the front door, that can and should be changed. If the bus loop is a constant source of confusion and frustration, that, too, can be dealt with by identifying and improving the processes that make up the system for the loading and unloading of buses. A cafeteria that is not an inviting place *can* become a warm, welcoming destination for everyone in the building. What is needed in all these circumstances is *the collective will to do something about it*. What is needed is a team committed to finding root causes and empowered to make the necessary process improvements. The status quo can be sent packing; *it is necessary that someone show it the door.*

Chapter 1: Going Viral With Improvement

Before starting any continuous-improvement journey, we need to take a look at where we are at this moment in time. What constitutes success? How is it measured, and how do *we measure up* in our classrooms, and in our school as a whole? Who are the key players in this drive for improvement, and do they understand their roles in the journey? What do administrators, faculty, staff, and students think about the school and the direction in which it is headed? The idea here is that leadership teams need to take the time to determine what excellence should look like, and then determine where the school is now, relative to where they want to go. This commitment to continuous improvement can—and should—spread to every corner of every building on campus, and to every facet of school life.

Chapter 2: Change and the Status Quo

Once we know where we are, along with where we want to go, how will we get there? What are the processes that will allow us to initiate and sustain forward movement? What are the forces and barriers holding us back, and how can they be overcome? What are the communication aspects of all this; who communicates what to whom along the way, and in such a way that it does not add to the perceived problems associated with change and the disruption of the status quo? How can administrators and other building leaders model process improvement? How do we make certain everyone is part of the effort, from students to administrators? In this chapter, we'll deal with these questions and many others that are related to the changes that are critical components of the continuous-improvement process.

Chapter 3: School Environment as Accelerant

Administrators and leadership teams within the building can accelerate forward movement on the continuous-improvement highway by actively supporting efforts at systemic improvement. While creating and sustaining a true professional learning community (PLC) offers the best hope for progress in the schoolhouse, teacher leaders or administrators not in a position to create a fully functioning schoolwide PLC can nevertheless support and encourage the development of individual or grade-level efforts at improving the organization. In this chapter, we'll also look at what can be done to enlist support staff in a schoolwide improvement effort.

Chapter 4: Classroom Environment as Accelerant

Building-level attempts at improvement aside, nothing changes in the classroom *unless something changes in the classroom*. Individual teachers can accelerate change or inhibit it. Students—the reason we're all here in the first place—depend on classroom leadership to make progress; teachers need to figure out what kind of classroom environment will accelerate forward progress for all students. This progress should be relentless, and classrooms need to be places where teachers and students feel comfortable in taking the risks and making the mistakes that make improvement possible.

Chapter 5: Systematizing Process Improvement in the Classroom

We get so caught up in content and testing that we sometimes fail to look at the processes that make learning and improvement possible. In this chapter, we'll look at building- and classroom-level processes that are critical components of systemic improvement. At the building level, leadership teams might ask, "How do we communicate with staff?" and, "Is that communication effective, and how do we know that?" At the classroom level, teachers might ask, "How do I deliver content?" and, "How do I know if those delivery systems are effective?" Effective processes are at the heart of continuous improvement, and we'll look at ways to harness their power in the name of progress and results by creating classroom systems that work.

Chapter 6: Facilitating the Long Haul

How do administrators, teachers, and staff know if they are being successful in an ongoing pursuit of academic and organizational excellence? What signposts along the way speak to our relative progress? In the classroom, what role does formative assessment play in ramping up improvement? What role does feedback from students, teachers, parents, and support staff play in all this? In this chapter, we'll explore ways to facilitate forward movement and to gauge progress along the continuous-improvement highway. To borrow from the sports realm, continuous improvement is not a sprint; it is a marathon, and one that really has no finish line.

Chapter 7: Not Waiting for the "Go!"

While it would be wonderful if every school district examined the status quo and then made the changes in processes and systems that would guarantee substantive and continuous forward progress, this is not always the case. It is not necessary, however, to wait for the starter pistol or the grand parade that begins the great push forward; leadership teams, grade-level teams, process-improvement teams, and individual supervisors and classroom teachers can all take stock of where they are now, where they want to go, and what it will take to get there. Continuous improvement is possible at every level in the organization, and such improvement can be generated and sustained by committed people working together or individually.

Chapter 8: Asking Questions and Getting Started

In this final chapter, we will discover ways to get started on the road to developing a continuous-improvement system. Out of the gate, perhaps the best way to approach improvement is to begin to ask questions. Teachers, for example, should continually question the efficacy of content-delivery methods. They might ask themselves, "Am I giving students enough quality feedback?" A process-improvement team focusing on customer service might ask, "What, exactly, is good customer service?" We'll also take a look at what the continuous-improvement cycle (Plan–Do–Study–Act) might look like in the classroom.

In classrooms at all levels, I am struck by teachers who consistently believe they *can* get better at what they do. The really great teachers working today instill in Eddie that same desire to *want* to do today what he could not do yesterday. Eddie needs to see that his teachers are willing to take risks on his behalf; he needs to see that his teachers treat mistakes—his and theirs—as feedback on the road to progress; he needs to see teachers who are relentlessly and transparently trying to improve what *they* do in an effort to improve what *he* does, no matter the obstacles and difficulties. Covington (1992) says that "the greatest legacy of education is to encourage a will to learn and to continue learning as personal circumstances change—in short, to promote a capacity for resiliency and self-renewal" (p. 4). A teacher who consistently demonstrates a will to learn and a capacity for self-renewal is modeling for her students that which will serve *them* well in adulthood.

Finally, I have seen educators who seem to sleepwalk through their own careers, and for whom "whatever" is a battle cry. I have observed administrators whose idea of the perfect status quo is a quiet building, polished floors, and an orderly lunchroom. I have nothing against polished floors or orderly lunchrooms, but organizational improvement involves vibrant discussions among teachers, staff, and students who are dedicated to disassembling the status quo in favor of relentless forward progress. Active classrooms with engaged students require those students to talk, share, and collaborate along the continuous-improvement highway.

Let's take to the road ourselves, therefore, as we look closely at the art and science of continuous improvement.

Acknowledgments

In the summer of 1996, I moved from my position as the middle school social studies coordinator for the Virginia Beach City Public Schools (VBCPS) to a new job as a trainer and coordinator in what would become the Office of Organizational Development. I thank Dr. Tim Jenney, superintendent at that time, and his assistant superintendent for curriculum and instruction, Mike O'Hara, for making that move possible.

The years between 1996 and my retirement from Virginia Beach in 2007 were simply wonderful from a growth standpoint, and I was able to meet and communicate with dozens of business and educational leaders involved with the search for quality. I was lucky enough to serve three outstanding directors during those years, leaders with limitless energy and vision: Debbie Gentry, Caryl Felty, and Olwen Herron. I thank them for providing our office with superb leadership and an understanding of what continuous improvement is about. I would also like to acknowledge Stephanie Enzmann for her help with Appendix A on building-level improvements.

Thanks to the following teachers for their contributions to this book: Hallie Antweil, Jeff Carrus, Sarah Erschabek, Kathy Galford, Joe Gentry, Scott McKenzie, Cindy Waldman, and Joy White. I also thank Karen O'Meara for her invaluable contribution to Appendix B. As always, I gratefully thank my Corwin Editor, Hudson Perigo, for her guidance, assistance, and encouragement. Working with everyone at Corwin is a pleasure, and I thank them all.

Finally, my wife, Candy, continues to support and encourage me in my new vocation as author, workshop facilitator, and consultant. I thank her first, last, and always.

Publisher's Acknowledgments

Corwin wishes to acknowledge the following peer reviewers for their editorial insight and guidance.

Lori Bird, Director

Center for Mentoring & Induction

Minnesota State University, Mankato

Mankato, MN

Kathleen Hwang, Principal

Sanders Corner Elem. School

Ashburn, VA

About the Author

 **Ron Nash** is the author of the Corwin (2008) bestseller *The Active Classroom*, a book dedicated to shifting students from passive observers to active participants in their own learning. Ron's professional career in education has included teaching social studies at the middle and high school levels. He also served as an instructional coordinator and organizational development specialist for the Virginia Beach City Public Schools for thirteen years. In that capacity, Ron trained thousands of teachers and other school-division employees in such varied topics as classroom management, instructional strategies, presentation techniques, relationship building, customer service, and process management. After Ron's retirement from the Virginia Beach City Public Schools in 2007, he founded Ron Nash and Associates, Inc., a company dedicated to working with teachers in the area of brain-compatible learning. Originally from Pennsylvania, Ron and his wife Candy, a French teacher, have lived in Virginia Beach for the past twenty-six years. Ron can be reached through his website at www.ronnashandassociates.com.

Prologue

As the last of several school buses pulled away from the parking lot and headed for neighborhoods all over town, one of Julie's students stood in the back window, smiling and slowly waving. Julie smiled, remembering how often that particular seventh grader had located and stepped on her last nerve during the school year. But it was June now, and the staff of Julie's middle school had just finished waving goodbye to all the kids in all the buses at noon on this last day of school for students. As that last bus disappeared around the corner of the building, there was a moment of silence—then a mighty cheer welcomed the arrival of summer. It was high fives all around, and the teachers headed for their cars and lunch on their own.

Becky, another seventh-grade teacher on Julie's four-person Falcon Team, approached her and said, "Are you coming with us to lunch?"

"You go ahead, Becky," said Julie. "I made a small cake last night, and I'll treat the team to dessert when you return."

Frowning slightly, Becky said, "Are you okay?"

Julie smiled and said, "I'm fine. Really, I just want to sit and think for a bit. I'll see you when you get back. We can have the cake in my classroom."

"Sounds good to me. See you later," said Becky. "We'll be at our usual haunt for lunch if you change your mind."

"Thanks," replied Julie.

Becky went toward the teacher parking lot, leaving Julie on the sidewalk by the bus loop. There was a small wooden bench with a dedication plate to a former teacher along the walkway into the building; the weather was sunny and warm, and the truth was that Julie needed to be alone for a few minutes. She needed to think, and she went back into the building, heading for the teacher's lounge. She reached into the refrigerator and retrieved a sandwich and a seedless orange, along with a bottle of water. Then she walked back to the bench near where the buses had pulled out just a few minutes before.

Julie had been teaching at this middle school for three years, and she had just received a continuing contract. At this point in her career, her future seemed assured—except for the minor fact that she was not sure she was succeeding for and with her students. The kids changed each year, of course, but she was keenly aware that this third year of teaching looked pretty much like the first and second years. The social studies curriculum was dictated by the district, based on state standards. This meant, of course, that the *what* was prescribed but the *how* of what she did was up to her—and this is where she was beginning to think the problem, if there was one, lay.

What little feedback she received on a daily, weekly, and yearly basis told her she was a pretty good teacher. Her summary evaluations had been good, but the standard district evaluation was in the form of a checklist that told her little. She was observed each quarter in her first year, and twice in her second and third years. During her first year in the classroom, her teacher mentor had told her his door was always open, and if she had questions she should not hesitate to track him down to get answers. Again, all this resulted in little in the way of feedback, and to someone like Julie who honestly wanted to get better at the *how* of teaching, this lack of substantive feedback was the basis for more than a little frustration on her part.

So here she was on this beautiful early-June afternoon, sitting on a bench and wondering how to go about getting better at her chosen profession. There was no question of not returning for a fourth year; she had signed a contract, and she would physically return in August. As she took a bite of her sandwich, Julie came to the conclusion that she must take the time this summer to explore ways to become a better teacher. She was aware that there was no systemic, organizational approach to improvement evident in her middle school; summary evaluations were it, and they provided Julie with little in the way of the kind of constructive feedback she might need to identify strengths and weaknesses, and make changes.

Still, Julie could find time to reflect on those past three years and ask herself why she thought she had been less than effective. She could look at test results, along with the quality of the essays she had her students write on a consistent basis. Was *she* providing enough feedback for her students? A winter workshop had introduced her to the comparative value of formative and summative assessments; should *she* be using more formative assessment pieces? Julie realized vaguely that she was doing too much work, and her students too little. What made her think that? She munched on a segment of her orange and came to the realization that a good deal of personal reflection was in the works for her this summer.

She also determined to bring together her Falcon Team partners in an attempt to pick their brains and do a little collective reflection as it related to the team itself. Julie was not the most experienced member of the team, but the others seemed to look up to her on occasion, and perhaps it was time for them to look at how they did what they did as a team. Each of them had strengths and weaknesses in terms of their approach to teaching and their methods of delivery, and those different perspectives might make for some powerful group reflection, assuming Julie could get them all together for an extended block of time.

Of her three teammates on the seventh-grade Falcon Team, one was retiring. This was, in her opinion, just as well; he was one of the most negative people Julie had ever met, and it was one reason she did not want to go to lunch with them today. He would be complaining about the weather, the curriculum, the parents, the color of the paint on the walls in his classroom, the administrators, and, most annoyingly to Julie, the students. This man really did not like kids much, and the kids knew it. Hopefully, his replacement would be someone with whom everyone could work, and whose attitude would reside somewhere outside the depths of despair. The mood would lift with his departure, and Julie looked forward to meeting a new math teacher in July.

Becky, the English teacher on the Falcon Team, would begin her second year in August, and she was extremely positive. Their fourth teammate, Yolanda, was an excellent science teacher and had taught Julie much in the three years they had been together. All in all, then, this coming year should be better, but Julie was still going to focus on how to become a better teacher. If the school's administrative leadership or the entire Falcon Team was willing to put into place a continuous-improvement model of some sort, so much the better; regardless, Julie was determined to turn her classroom into a more learning-centered environment. During the school year that had just ended, a really supportive assistant principal had arranged for Julie to visit the class-room of an outstanding seventh-grade social studies teacher at another middle school in the district. She had been amazed at how much the students had accomplished in that fifty-minute class, and she deter-mined to begin her continuous-improvement efforts with a phone call to that teacher this afternoon. Julie would invite her to lunch, in hopes of picking her brain and getting some advice.

Julie truly loved her students, and she enjoyed teaching social studies, but she determined that this fourth year would be different. She would try to put into place a system of some sort that would accelerate improvement for her and for her seventh graders. She was convinced that this continuous-improvement journey would also guarantee that she would continue to enjoy teaching, while better serving those students in her care. Before the status quo became a comfortable rut for Julie, as appeared to be the case for some other teachers in her building, she would make some changes in the way she approached the *how* of what she did.

1

Going Viral With Improvement

I once saw a school cafeteria manager who wore a funny hat. The cafeteria manager with the funny hat *greeted every student in the lunch line by name*. This man works in a school dedicated to continuous improvement. The principal of the school involves her staff in the continuous-improvement process, but the idea of progress is nonnegotiable. At this school, problems are identified, solutions are surfaced, and evaluation comes close on the heels of implementation. All this takes place in the context of a continuous-improvement journey that never ends. Process is king, and the blame game is out of bounds.

I could have begun this first chapter with a classroom-based story; I could have chosen many just from this particular elementary school, Sanders Corner, in Loudoun County, Virginia. In dynamic schools like this, however, progress is not limited to the classroom, and everyone in the school is a player. In terms today's web-obsessed generation can well understand, when improvement goes viral in a school or district, *everyone is involved*. In the case of the cafeteria manager with the funny hat, the kids liked the hat and loved the idea that he cared enough to get to know their names. I can also report that this particular cafeteria manager, Nick DeCicco (Mr. Nick to the kids), is constantly working to upgrade the quality of the food and service for the kids in his care. He talked with me about what they were doing in the cafeteria—and he spoke the language of improvement.

DeCicco began his tenure at Sanders Corner Elementary School with several goals: improving efficiency in the areas of the cost and quality of food; building positive relationships with staff, students, and parents; and making the school cafeteria a fun place to be. After many months of making changes and adjustments, DeCicco related to his sister that "something magic was happening" in the school cafeteria. He knew this because he was at the point of sale in the lunch line every day (not in his office), wearing a smile and one of those funny hats—and greeting each student by name. I observed this firsthand one morning, and I, too, saw the magic. Those elementary students love "Mr. Nick," and I watched their faces light up when he greeted them in the lunch line. With the active support of a school principal who understands there is nothing that can't be made better, DeCicco set about improving every aspect of every process connected to a system he understood would benefit his primary clients—the students of Sanders Corner Elementary.

Continuous improvement is not a destination; it is a journey that really has no finish line. The idea is to put in place a system that will outlast the tenure of a particular principal. The active components of this system are processes that are put in place to deal with and solve problems that might otherwise impede progress. For example, in the school I referenced in the opening paragraphs, the principal, Kathy Hwang, empowered the faculty to solve the problem of hallways that had become noisy enough to negatively affect learning in classrooms all over the building. The faculty agreed on a solution and then implemented it. They came back together to report on its efficacy, and that process is still in place three years later. I can attest to the fact that the hallways are quiet, and teachers can continue with lessons uninterrupted. The problem was surfaced by the faculty, and the solution came from the faculty; this serves to support the notion that those closest to the problems are often closest to the solutions. This improvement was not a top-down decree from the principal's office. The faculty invested in the dialogue surrounding the problem, and they bought into the agreed-upon process that ultimately solved it. True to the spirit of continuous improvement, the process is consistently revisited to see if further adjustments are needed to ensure its continued efficacy.

The Very First Thing

We'll talk later about the whole idea of change, but suffice it to say here that veteran teachers can perhaps be forgiven for being skeptical and even cynical about the latest change initiative passed down from the powers that be. My experience tells me that even the most skeptical and cynical veteran teachers were not always so. Part of the reason for their reluctance to jump on board what seems to them to be the program du jour is that improvement initiatives are often introduced with great fanfare (and often with great expenditure), only to be abandoned after a few months or years. Some of these initiatives die the death of a thousand cuts, as teachers and staff who were not part of the original decision begin to spot the flaws and problems as the initiative unfolds. Administrators at the building level receive pushback that they may, in turn, push back up the ladder, and people in the district's central office begin to feel the pressure from what could be dozens of schools. At some point, a decision may be made to jettison the program altogether, and scores of believers become skeptics, while scores of skeptics move to the ranks of the cynics. The whole thing leaves a bad taste in the collective mouth of the organization, and another opportunity for positive change and improvement is lost.

This leads us to the very first thing administrators at any level need to do: *Commit to putting in place a system of improvement that will outlive you.* Too many administrators try to be "the answer person." By this I mean that when teachers or other employees approach the principal, he immediately provides the answer to their questions. It is as if the principal has a mental briefcase full of answers; all that needs to be done is to find the right answer from the briefcase, and the staff member walks away happy (or not)—*but no closer to being able to solve problems on her own or with others in any collegial way.* Have a question? Go find the principal. One problem here, of course, is that when the principal leaves, *the solution-to-the-problems briefcase goes with him.* Everyone on staff then hopes that whatever else the *new* principal is or is not, he or she has a briefcase full of answers. The more critical problem is that the staff is no closer to being able to build a capacity to solve problems on their own. They have come to rely totally on "the powers that be" for answers and solutions. Any principal about to retire ought to be able to do so without worrying about what will happen to the staff and students. If members of the staff have the capacity to walk confidently down the continuous-improvement highway, the retirement of the principal will not be an impediment to forward progress; the system for steady and effective improvement is in place and functioning.

The best principals I know are everywhere in the building. They observe classrooms, talk with custodians, interact with teachers, and know the names of scores and even hundreds of students. I know principals who read to students, and I know principals who have students read to them. They love what they do, and they have enormous reserves of energy. Most of all, they know how to harness the power of the human beings in the building in the search for progress. Some things may be negotiable for these principals, but one thing that is *not* negotiable is the drive to improve. Putting in place the mechanisms for continuous improvement requires an understanding that wherever one is as a teacher, paraprofessional, secretary, custodian, school bus driver, or cafeteria worker—*there is always a need to get better.*

The Role of Leadership

From the beginning of any conscious effort at organizational improvement, everyone from the front office to the classroom to the cafeteria must understand that the continuous-improvement journey has no end, and that is as it should be. As Smylie (2010) reminds us, improvement is not just about change. Something can change for the worse or for the better, so "improvement requires change in the direction toward some valued objective." He continues,

> To be sure, there is progress to be made, successes to be attained, and objectives to be met. But improvement in the sense of continuous improvement is never fully achieved. The valued outcome is the organization getting better and better and better at what it is, at what it does, and what it achieves, ad infinitum. It is the stance that good is never good enough. (p. 25)

This idea of no finish line is sometimes difficult for employees in an organization to understand. "Never good enough" is not something people long to hear, but leaders need to invest the time necessary to help everyone understand that it is not about good or bad, or right or wrong; it is about moving inexorably forward from a baseline—wherever or whatever that baseline is.

There is no one—teacher, administrator, secretary, custodian, or cafeteria worker—who cannot improve over time. Customer service in the front office can always be improved, positive changes can always be made in the way the building is cleaned and maintained, improvements in connection with the lunchroom are always possible, instruction can be made better—improvements in all these areas make the school more efficient and productive. A common belief that continuous-improvement efforts are desirable will make the building a more pleasant place to be. Employees who pay attention to their external customers and their internal customers will help move the organization steadily down the continuous-improvement highway.

Whom Do We Serve?

Efforts at continuous improvement often come not as part of some master plan, but as a realization that no matter what our job is in the schoolhouse, there are those whom we serve externally (students, parents, community) and internally (colleagues). Those who greet parents and students in the front office also interact with members of the administration, faculty, and support staff. I have observed front office personnel who treat absolutely everyone with courtesy and undivided attention, and I have seen office personnel smile at parents and then snap at employees, all in the space of a few minutes. What-ever standard of customer service is in place for external customers ought to be in place for everyone else in the building, for the simple reason that a double standard in this area can be detrimental to the organization.

While teaching social studies at a middle school in the early 1990s, I was also the yearbook adviser. Anyone who has held that job under-stands that a great deal of time is spent after school and into the eve-ning in an attempt to make the book worthy of publication. Working late, therefore, I often had the opportunity to chat with the night custodian. Early in the school year, she sat down and asked me what she could do to make my job easier. I thought for a moment and then suggested some things having to do with what part of the board to erase, furniture placement, and so on. Appreciating that she had taken the time to solicit my feedback, I returned the favor by asking what I could do to assist her. She came up with two or three things that would help in the efficiency department, and from that moment on, we both went out of our way to assist one another. This night custo-dian understood that I was her internal customer; she was invested in making my classroom a better place for me and my students.

While her efforts on my behalf were laudatory, and much appreciated by me, it was not part of an overall program of continuous improvement in the building. It happened because we both came to understand the supportive relationship between us. After forty years in education, I could mention scores of employees who acted in the spirit of improving how they did what they did on their own, with no direction from above. The problem with this, of course, is that these individual efforts are not part of a system of improvement; they are isolated incidents, and unlikely to move the organization forward in any meaningful way.

Let's suppose for a moment that the head day and night custodians, along with several teacher leaders, administrators, and other support staff within the building, could be brought together every month from August until May in a succession of two-hour sessions. The expressed purpose of these meetings would be to look closely at what is working in terms of building maintenance and to surface areas in need of improvement. Meetings like that would not be about right or wrong, or good or bad, or about playing the blame game; they would be concerned with *where we are now and where we want to go.* In facilitated meetings with custodians, teachers, and staff, what my night custodian and I had agreed to as it related to my classroom might very well have been set as the standard for every room in the building. Those meetings—dedicated to how the custodial staff and the other adults in the building could help each other—might have moved us all forward. Monthly work sessions with this same group would have gone a long way toward systematizing the sporadic improvement efforts of a few people in the building—and, importantly, everything decided upon in those sessions would have benefitted the students in our care.

In a profession where the continuous improvement of students is a given, the adults in the building ought to model for students the same methodology for success over time. Students should *see* teachers and staff collaborating on problem-solving techniques, taking risks on behalf of kids, and accepting inevitable mistakes as feedback—all in the name of moving confidently down the continuous-improvement highway. Modeling collaboration in the name of improvement is powerful.

This brings us to the second requirement for administrators who seek to put in place an improvement system that will outlive them: *Involve everyone at every level from day one.* Any serious attempt at systemically and continuously improving a school or school district must begin with involvement from those who have a stake in the outcome. Totally top-down efforts and improvement invariably lead to pushback; it then becomes a matter of how much pushback the administrators who introduced the initiative can take before they throw up their hands and call an end to it. If staff is expected to implement reform efforts, they should be directly involved from the start. The whole improvement effort must be utterly, completely, and consistently transparent in every way.

Those Closest to the Problem

One important role, then, of building leadership is to work to set in place processes (the monthly meetings we just described, for instance) dedicated to building the capacity of the adults in the schoolhouse to identify and solve their own problems. It is not the job of the administrators to simply provide all the answers or even to ask all the relevant *questions.* Those monthly meetings should continue even if the principal retires or transfers elsewhere in the district. Even in the absence of the principal, those in attendance can ask the right questions and seek corresponding solutions. Process-improvement teams should be empowered to make decisions when possible, so that the good work goes on no matter who is principal; there is always work to do because there are always problems in search of processes, and there are always processes in search of improvement.

Anyone who wants to find out what is right and wrong with a school from the viewpoint of faculty need look no further than the faculty lounge or the parking lot. To the casual observer, a school may appear clean and well run, but every organization has processes that break down in practice, attempts at communication that go awry, inefficiencies that are clear to everyone, complaints in search of an outlet, and problems crying out for solutions. To this extent, schools are no different than any other organization. As in any organization, the people who are closest to the problems may be in the best position to surface ideas and solutions. When it comes to improving the school in order to better serve its primary customers—students, parents, and the community at large—a building principal has an important and perhaps unique perspective, yet it is one perspective among many in any potentially effective improvement process.

Of one thing I am certain: Concerns, problems, and outright complaints *will surface* in the school building. The question is, will they surface in a controlled way, as the result of a systemic approach to problem solving, or will they surface at random wherever teachers gather in the parking lot, or chat on cell phones or at computer keyboards? Great principals regularly surface concerns and then enlist everyone's help in dealing with those concerns or solving those problems. Effective principals involve staff in the decision-making process. Top-down improvement efforts instituted without buy-in from those directly affected may flounder down the road, and this is true with any organization.

A Matter of Perspective

A business acquaintance and I were once discussing the whole issue of continuous improvement, and he told me of a bank whose upper management team decided they would improve customer service by installing a very efficient telephone-answering system to replace the person who had always answered the phone and transferred the calls. The problem, of course, was that *customers really liked talking to the wonderful lady who used to answer the phone as the first point of contact.* Unfortunately for the bank, no one thought to ask the customers about this *before* the system was installed and before the (considerable) expenditures had been made in support of the new system. The outcry against this change was so loud and widespread that the bank was forced to scrap the new, efficient telephone-answering system, and replace it with the nice lady who loved talking to customers. The higher management of the bank, of course, put efficiency above what the customers loved—and never sought feedback from them or from the employees at ground level in the bank. At the upper managerial level of a bank, efficiency may be of primary concern; to customers—and to the employees who have to deal with those customers on a daily basis—the personal touch, a smile, and a bit of light banter might well be what customers want. In short, management simply thought like management and not like customers; this lack of empathy led to disastrous results.

For years I facilitated workshops on customer service for school-district employees, and I asked the following question: How many of you would prefer to have a person answer the phone when you call a company, rather than a machine? In every single case, almost every hand went up. Almost every hand, every time. Hardly scientific, I know, but telling nonetheless. Every reader, I suspect, has a horror story about being on hold for an inordinate amount of time, waiting to speak to a person. My personal record is twenty-three minutes—twenty-three minutes I'll never get back. Imagine being the person who sits there all day long, answering the phone for customers who have spent a good chunk of their lives waiting to talk to them.

If organizations, including schools and districts, were to conduct surveys of parents (customers), businesses (customers), and other community members (customers), those organizations might come to the conclusion that stakeholders might prefer to have a happy, attentive, alert person actually answer the phone, rather than have to punch buttons and deal with an unnecessary rise in blood pressure. Decisions as to how to treat members of the school community (teachers, paraprofessionals, classified employees, parents) might best be arrived at with the help of those very people—stakeholders all. Decisions made by one or two people in an administrative office—the product of one or two sets of eyes—may not be effective over time; a commitment to continuous improvement requires the direct involvement of those who are most affected by the results. Their input results in better outcomes, smoother processes . . . and happier campers.

The Search for Feedback

Any principal or leadership team willing to put a facilitator and representative stakeholders together long enough to surface perceived strengths and weaknesses in the system may well find other critical areas in need of improvement: among them communication, communication, and—oh yes—communication. If there is any single barrier to improvement more critical—or potentially damaging—than effective communication, I'm not certain what it might be.

The principal who thinks his skills as a communicator make him particularly effective in that regard may be surprised to learn that others disagree, but he will only discover that if feedback is sought through a working group, survey, or dozens of conversations intended to solicit feedback from employees. Here is something I know for certain: Unless leadership makes an effort to surface feedback through a regular process, the feedback will surface in the faculty lounge, the hallways, and the parking lot. School administrators may never hear it or see it, but it will be there—*and it will not contribute in any way to continuous improvement.*

In the process of purposefully soliciting feedback on any number of issues, building administrators can practice that communication skill so often lacking in organizations today: listening. Employees in buildings (and students in classrooms) where it appears that no one in charge is listening may not share what is on their minds, except with their peers. (Stand in a lunchroom full of students for half an hour, or in a faculty lounge full of teachers.) Communicating effectively is not just about great articulation and clarity in the written and spoken word; it is about focusing on an employee, listening intently and purposefully to what she has to say, and seeking understanding in the form of paraphrasing or asking pertinent questions. It is also about taking the time afterwards to reflect on what that employee said, and getting back to her later on in order to make certain both the administrator and employee (or teacher and student) are on the same sheet of music.

Administrators who understand the balance between talking and listening in professional relationships are on their way to improving their own communication skills and defusing potential problems that arise because of a lack of communication or understanding. Teachers would do well to adopt this same balance between the amount of time they spend talking to students and the amount of time they spend listening to what students have to say; this is a great relationship builder any way one looks at it. Effective communication is the lifeblood of continuous improvement. Developing and using powerful listening skills is a critically important part of any communication system.

Improving Processes While Supporting Learning

It is my experience that large teams of building-level employees do not work as efficiently in collaborative efforts as smaller teams. The more people there are in a working group, the harder it is to get everyone together, and the sheer size of the group may make efficient process facilitation difficult for the person running the meetings and coordinating the input and output of the group. As one who has facilitated dozens of teams, I can report that small teams are easier to manage, and communication is less cumbersome. Ultimately, the size of the team is less important than what is accomplished in the time allotted. As long as there are multiple perspectives on the team, representing every point of view, much can be accomplished.

The focus of any team should always be on learning. Every process in the building can be looked at in terms of how it affects students and their own continuous-improvement efforts as supported by the adults in the building. Small teams can be assembled in order to put the microscope on how—and how effectively—things are done. Conzemius and O'Neill (2002) describe process-improvement teams as those that "exist to improve any process in the school or system that, because of inefficiencies or unnecessary bureaucracy,

[has] the potential to divert resources away from the district's core mission of student learning" (p. 31). The team meets, dissects a particular process, evaluates how it furthers the district's emphasis on student learning, and if necessary, streamlines the process.

Let's suppose, for example, that four new teachers arrived at a particular middle school at the beginning of the last school year. In this instance, three of them came on board before July 1, and while the fourth was not actually hired until the beginning of August, building administrators knew who would be in which classrooms by July 1. My experience has been that new teachers are often tremendously excited about seeing and setting up their new classrooms, but there may be a process-based impediment to making that happen: Specifically, and traditionally, the building's custodial staff cleaned, waxed, and otherwise prepared the classrooms in a certain order during the course of the summer months, as defined by their own needs and priorities. Therefore, the classrooms of the new teachers may not ordinarily have priority for cleaning.

During the five in-service days prior to the start of school, the mentors for these four new teachers noticed that their protégés seemed stressed out because of everything that needed to be done before the students reported the following Monday. In meetings with the mentors, two of the protégés lamented the fact that in the midst of everything else that was going on—meetings, professional development, trips downtown to HR, setting up electronic gradebooks, and so on—they did not get enough time to really set their classrooms up the way they would have liked. What could have been a very relaxed and enjoyable process on their part was less so because of everything else that came their way during that busy teachers' week.

Looking ahead to the *next* school year, the mentors, meeting with the assistant principal who worked most closely with them and with their protégés, suggested that a process-improvement team be assembled to take a look at the order in which the classrooms were cleaned during the summer months. The head custodian, along with one of the teacher mentors, the assistant principal, and one of the four new teachers all met in a small conference room in order to see if something could be done to get the rooms for new teachers ready prior to next August 1, so that new teachers hired prior to that date had some unencumbered time to set up the classrooms as they wished well prior to the first day teachers had to report back. The team began by looking at the process the custodians used in order to ensure that the classrooms were ready by that teachers' week. With some adjustments to that schedule, the head custodian was able to talk with his staff and arrange for those particular rooms to be done first, along with the cleaning of those particular student desks and the other furniture in those rooms. The members of this process-improvement team also agreed that this adjusted process would be revisited the following September by this same team (with the addition of one of the new teachers who was able to take advantage of the improved process), in order to assess its effectiveness.

The key to making the decision was the belief that getting these particular rooms cleaned and waxed early would reduce some of the attendant confusion that brand new teachers are bound to feel during teachers' week. While it might result in an adjustment to what was a time-honored room-preparation process, the potential benefit to learning outweighed the understandable desire to maintain a status quo that worked for the custodians during the summer. That same process-improvement team might very well look at other things that could be done for new teachers that would assist their transition into the school community. This particular process-improvement team was composed of those with the most investment in the possible outcomes: the custodians who cleaned the rooms and "owned" the current process, the mentors who worked more closely than anyone else with their protégés, the administrator who worked with both the mentors and the new teachers, and one of the new teachers who now had nearly a year under her belt and who could speak most eloquently to the pressures of that first week. Going forward, the assistant principal's task was to keep the head custodian informed concerning the number of new teachers and the rooms into which they would be assigned. Armed with this information, the custodians could make the adjustments that resulted in those classrooms being ready to go prior to August 1, a full two weeks before teachers reported.

There may be other teams, according to Conzemius and O'Neill (2002), that are formed in the name of improvement. Instruction-related teams (departmental or grade level) may deal with services that directly benefit students, steering teams that deal with major initiatives, and school-level improvement teams that are "stewards of the school's mission vision, and core values" (p. 26). Every one of these teams, large or small, is dedicated to improving systems and instruction in the building. Parents, as Conzemius and O'Neill affirm, may be sought for these teams, and "this is especially true when the outcome of the team's work is likely to require community support . . . or involves any decision having significant impact on student learning"

(p. 27). The composition of any improvement team should be careful to include those closest to the issue, problem, or process.

The Benefits of Success

As it is with students, small successes can lead to an increase in the confidence and feeling of competence that can pave the way for future success in identifying and solving problems, improving instruction as part of a grade-level or department-level effort, and streamlining and improving processes and systems. The point at which it begins to go viral in the building is the point at which employees—instructional, administrative, or support—begin to see the positive effects of decisions made on their behalf, and in support of students and parents, and may be more willing to assist in the overall continuous-improvement process.

An example of this might be a school-improvement team that decides to survey the school community in order to find out what the perceptions are regarding how well the school is doing in the areas of safety, instruction, school–home communication, and first impressions when people enter the building. The survey is developed with the assistance of the district-level accountability office, and it is administered, collected, and analyzed so that everyone in the building can get an idea of just how the community perceives the school. The results of this initial survey can function as a baseline that will help inform decision making as they move forward in the various areas covered by the survey. One year later, that same survey might well show some interesting contrasts from the established baseline; if the perceptions improved overall, or in specific areas, this can once again inform decision making for the third year. This feedback, provided year after year, or at least every couple of years, can greatly assist schools in the continuous-improvement process. Again, demonstrable success leads to more demonstrable success, and the whole school moves forward.

Such surveys should be constructed carefully, and the persons constructing and distributing the survey should make certain they are free of leading questions. In districts that include an office or department devoted to accountability and testing, there may be testing specialists who can assist with survey development. The results of the survey should be made available to stakeholders, and any changes made on the basis of survey results should be communicated; the entire continuous-improvement effort should be well communicated and transparent. It has been my experience that few things are more frustrating than taking part in surveys that subsequently disappear down a black hole; those who take part in a survey and hear nothing are less likely to participate in such efforts down the road.

Walking the Walk at the Administrative Level

Any building administrator who wants her employees to hold up to the light *how* they do *what* they do on a daily basis must be willing to model how this might be done. There are plenty of processes that administrators can seek to streamline and, if necessary, replace with new processes. One example of this would be the whole nature and purpose of faculty meetings that are often devoted to providing information in a talking-head format, with one speaker after another going over "what people need to know," things that might be as easily handled by e-mails or other means. Building leadership teams can ensure that faculty meetings can instead be dynamic professional-development sessions where teachers and administrators examine data, share ideas and successes, and make decisions about changes that will move the school forward.

Another area rife with possibilities for accelerating improvement is the system of teacher evaluation that is in place in many schools. In these schools, administrators make one or two visits per year, and the summative evaluation finds its way into the teacher's mailbox or becomes part of a short administrator–teacher conversation at the end of the year—at which point the teacher and the administrator sign off on the evaluation form. It may be that the school district requires that form, but it is still possible for administrators to visit classrooms more frequently and to make the whole process more formative in nature. Observations can be followed by postobservation conversations that hone in on specific areas of improvement, as well as areas of strength. This would allow teachers to make adjustments as the year progresses, and might be part of a larger, overall improvement effort.

The willingness of building administrators to layer a formative process on top of a (required) summative process models for teachers the effectiveness of formative assessments in their own classrooms. Administrators could, in the fall of a given school year, pilot this formative process with several volunteers, evaluate the program, and then expand it schoolwide after the first of the year. The administrators and the volunteers can meet in order to gauge the effectiveness of the formative process. This examination of the effectiveness of the program should, in turn, model for teachers the value of looking at their own processes and systems as they move forward on their own continuous-improvement journeys.

Administrators who are seen walking the walk are much more likely to get the support of school employees for any continuous-improvement initiative. Just as students pick up quickly on inconsistencies in the classroom, teachers and other employees watch administrators closely to see if what they are *saying* matches what they are *doing*. A decided lack of congruence between words and actions can short-circuit continuous-improvement efforts. Administrators can model effective change and process improvement in ways that get the attention of everyone in the building. Employees need to see that leaders are willing to walk with them, listen to them, and work with them—rather than simply hand down decrees from the front office.

It is one thing for administrators to develop powerful listening skills in working with staff; it is another to lose sight of what is most important for the customers who count most—students. The narrow interests of individuals in the organization must give way to the overarching goal of improved instruction, increased efficiency, and customer service, for both external and internal customers. In many schools, the newest teachers are placed with students who are desperately in need of the most experienced and effective teachers. This often happens because veteran teachers want—and receive—the classes and students they request, and it is the new teachers who move into situations where they simply do not have the amount of expertise and experience necessary to succeed. Administrators and leadership teams need to make certain that efforts to improve instruction result in a matching of teachers and students that best serves the latter.

The Power of Reflection and Self-Evaluation

Empowered groups of stakeholders can do much to make forward progress on the continuous-improvement highway. With the success of students firmly in mind, individuals and small teams can accelerate overall improvement efforts from the front office to classroom. When, for example, teachers at the first-grade level meet with second-grade teachers in regular work sessions, they can work out exactly what is needed in terms of readiness when first graders make the transition to second grade. The basic understanding of both groups of teachers is that if first graders are not ready for second grade, the second-grade teachers have to account for that and make up lost ground for those students. If, however, vertical teams working in concert can dovetail their continuous-improvement efforts, students and teachers will both benefit. The great thing here is that grade-level teams in the elementary schools already exist; it remains for them to meet with one another on an ongoing basis toward one purpose: making certain that when students move to the next level, they are ready.

The key with vertical teams, as with all teams, is a willingness to lay it all out there and to receive and accept input from those with different perspectives. It may be tough for a fourth-grade teacher to hear from a fifth-grade colleague that many students are not coming to the higher grade with necessary grammatical skills. If that is the case, it is not a time to play the blame game; it is a time to involve grade-level teams from K through 5 in working on what needs to be done at each grade level in order to ensure that each year more and more students are up to speed in terms of grammar. In order for continuous improvement to go viral, teachers and employees need to understand that improvement is not about assigning blame or finding scapegoats; continuous improvement is about being willing to self-evaluate, honor other perspectives, accept feedback, and work with colleagues regularly, in continuous-improvement mode. As we will see later on, this involves taking a big step for teachers and other school employees used to working in isolation. A true and consistent continuous-improvement effort requires a willingness to break the grip of isolationism, work collaboratively toward common goals, and develop a system of improvement that will facilitate and accelerate the growth of the organization.

Final Thoughts

Being part of a successful improvement effort in one area will lead those involved to believe that it can be duplicated in another. Skeptics who observe that administrators are truly walking the walk can be turned into believers. For their part, administrators and other school leaders can act with a sense of urgency that keeps continuous improvement consistently on the front burner; they can also seek to involve all stakeholders in a process that is truly bottom-up, rather than top-down.

In Chapter 2, we'll explore change and the drag often induced by the status quo in schools.

2

Change and
the Status Quo

There are two words that will send people fleeing for the exits: *fire* and *change*. It is also my experience that there is a considerable— and critical—difference between what administrators *say* and what teachers and other employees *hear*. For example, let's suppose a building principal announces the following on Monday morning of the week teachers have returned from summer break.

Here is what the principal *said:*

Welcome back, everyone. I have some exciting news. The district is kicking off a great reform initiative that will, I have no doubt, lead to our school being a better place for all of us, students included. I have been assured that we will be taking this step-by-step, and it may be several years before everything that has been planned is put in place. The superintendent has personally told me we will start slowly, and sufficient support and substantial resource materials will be forthcoming. We'll talk more about this later this week, but I wanted you to know that together we will accomplish great things!

Here is what the staff may have *heard* in what the principal said:

Welcome back, everyone. We are going to disrupt the very fabric of your classroom, and the status quo as you know it is history. Whatever you are doing now is old news; the district has decided, without your input, to change the way you do what you do. I'm not sure I agree with what is speeding our way like an out-of-control freight train, but there isn't much I can do about it. Now, go back to your rooms and spend the next few days wondering what in the name of everything you hold dear this is all about.

Once again, there is what was *intended* and there is what was *perceived*, and the two can be miles apart. It was not the intent of the administrator to scare the bejeebers out of everyone, and members of the staff may not have communicated their concerns at the meeting, but that is only because they had not had time to process what they heard, then talk about it in the hallways, the parking lot, and the faculty lounge. It is there, and through a gazillion e-mails and over lunch that day, that what was communicated gets amplified, is partially understood or misunderstood, and begins to encounter pushback, even though no details have yet been released.

Administrators who truly want to ramp up the improvement process at any level are better off not treating the initiative like the dropping of the ball in Times Square on New Year's Eve. The pomp is not necessary; what is necessary is to understand fully that whatever it is teachers are doing in their classrooms, the system they have put in place there has evolved over time and now exists for them as the status quo. They have adjusted to the changes in the curriculum, a new group of kids every year, and maybe a change of classrooms now and then—but they have done this largely on their own and in relative isolation. When the next big thing comes along, they may well see it as an assault on that to which they have become accustomed.

One of the immutable laws of nature is that human beings have a marvelous capacity to adjust to circumstances while continuing to do pretty much what they have always done. There is a comforting sameness to what they are doing, and until a major initiative comes along, from their perspective, things proceed in a more-or-less predictable and acceptable fashion. The status quo is something to which they have adjusted, and these employees may react adversely to what may promise to be considerable and disruptive change, including continuous-improvement initiatives.

The Drag of the Status Quo

When these great initiatives are put in motion, they immediately collide with the status quo in the organization at every level. Everyone from the secretaries in the front office to the teachers in the classrooms have already come to an understanding with the status quo as it pertains to their areas of expertise. Teachers have their routines (and lessons) worked out, and custodians have spent years putting in place their version of the status quo, as have secretaries and cafeteria workers in the building. The way things are is the way things are, and it has become comfortable for all concerned. This applies to students as well; they have made their own adjustments to daily life in the classroom, hallways, and cafeteria, as well as in every other facet of their own version of the status quo. Grafting large chunks of change onto the accepted routines of everyone in the building can result in frustration and pushback from those affected by the changes.

In the classroom, for example, it may be that teachers attend a day-long seminar where it is made clear that they will begin to use checklists, rubrics, and a dozen other kinds of formative feedback—all within a few weeks of the beginning of school in the fall. Without fully understanding the why and how of these new concepts, teachers may be forced into working them into their daily routines quickly, leading to confusion, frustration, and pushback. The resulting chaos may also be felt by students confronted with new and unfamiliar strategies and concepts. Students may also push back in the classroom, and that leaves teachers caught between pressure from above (the powers that be) and below (confused kids). This often leads teachers to go negative, and faculty lounges can become hotbeds of general discontent as teachers complain and commiserate with one another in the face of this seemingly massive disruption of the status quo to which they have become accustomed.

Ramping Up Implementation

Fullan (2010) cautions administrators against trying to do too much too soon in terms of change, however necessary. "Do not load up on vision, evidence, and sense of urgency," says Fullan. "Rather, give people new experiences in relatively nonthreatening circumstances, and build on it" (p. 25). Teachers and other school personnel who are able to experience success with something relatively small and impactful that is introduced into their daily routine are much more likely to embrace the next round or the next step in the overall change process. I have known otherwise cynical teachers who enjoy the feeling that comes with success in some small area or aspect of their teaching. In the same way that *too much* and *too fast* won't last for students, the same can be said of their teachers. If employees in an organization decide that change is too expensive, they will push back; some may actively seek to sabotage the overall continuous-improvement program.

When it comes to continuous-improvement efforts at the district level, there is sometimes a tendency to concentrate on reconstructing an entire curriculum in order to make certain everyone (literally) is on the same page. Meetings are held, decisions are made, binders are filled, and marching orders go out from central office in a well-meaning attempt to jump-start improvement. Schmoker (2006) recalls working in a district where administrators "were convinced that the needs assessments and surveys and programs and book studies and action steps that filled the columns and boxes of our thick plans would have a palpable effect on instruction" (p. 35). Unfortunately, it turned out that these gargantuan planning efforts did not translate into improvement.

Massive improvement efforts often run headlong—and at great speed—into the bedrock nature of the status quo in classrooms all over the district. The teachers charged with instituting the change that everyone in central office is convinced will work may not see the value in making the changes; their comfort level with the way things are after many years of teaching (and being left alone all that time) leads to the dragging of feet. An administration that for years supported isolation now turns 180 degrees and suddenly insists on the way things are going to have to be. Worse, it may be clear—or it may become increasingly apparent as time passes—that building-level administrators are not fully supportive of the changes dictated from above. Having had little or no buy-in themselves, building-level administrative teams may be half-hearted in their efforts to support these changes beyond what is required and provided by central office.

Administrators and leadership teams charged with a new, district-level continuous-improvement initiative would do well to spend a good deal of time reflecting on the following:

- What will happen if we announce this massive effort on Day 1?
- Is it advisable, on reflection, to do away with the fanfare and grand announcements and simply work with teachers and groups of teachers and staff on various process-improvement projects?
- This is late June; what are teachers now texting and e-mailing to each other if they have heard something about what is coming?

- Is there something we need to communicate to our staff now, before they return? If so, what?
- If tradition and the status quo are powerful forces, how do we jump-start the improvement effort without seeming to disrupt those forces?
- If our commitment is to improving systems and processes in the schoolhouse, how can we be effective over time?
- Is it advisable to bring a few teachers in this summer, in order to work on some small improvement tasks (the system for dropping off and loading students in the bus loop, ways to provide planning time for teams and individuals as they seek to identify and improve systems and processes, strategies for reducing the amount of classroom lecture, etc.) that can be presented to staff when they return? If we did that, would those involved in that work and those decisions spread the word that this effort is aimed at getting better—that it is not *The Son of Fad du Jour?*
- Are there key teacher leaders that can be taken to lunch in order to reflect with them about how past improvement efforts may have misfired or collapsed over time, with an eye toward enlisting their help in how efforts at improvement can be made less threatening?
- Could a summer survey of teachers and staff solicit ideas for processes that might stand in need of improvement?

It may well be that if efforts at improving systems and processes can be up and working by the time teachers return to school, with some positive results already on the table, staff may be a great deal more receptive to more of the same. If administrators are willing to touch base with key teacher leaders in the building, it is possible that some of those teachers could hit the ground running with some classroom changes (more formative assessments, introduction of performance tasks, use of checklists and rubrics) that can be evaluated not too far into the school year. By taking a good deal of time in the summer to reflect on what needs to be done and then make some decisions, with the support of various teachers and support staff, that back-to-school week may be far less threatening, with a whole lot less anxiety.

It is important, no matter who is initiating the continuous-improvement effort, that administrators and employees sit down to talk about why it is that efforts like this sometimes fail. This gives key members of the staff a chance to think about their thinking in a very reflective—and nonthreatening—atmosphere. The idea is to identify obstacles that might get in the way and agree on ways to remove them. If communication in all its aspects has been a problem in the past, how is it possible to turn that negative into a positive? Here is a critical question: If teachers have felt threatened by, or out of step with, previous improvement efforts, *how can that be avoided this time around?* All this is process; it is something that needs to be dealt with up front, before moving forward, and everything needs to be transparent as it unfolds.

Accelerating Improvement Through Modeling

It has been my experience that professional development sessions often amount to telling teachers what they should be doing. Often, at the beginning of a major instructional initiative, teachers drag themselves to two- or four-hour seminars where one talking head after another walks them through page after page of plans, the creation of which involved none of the teachers present at the session. Teachers leave with a binder and the assurance that if all unfolds as planned, teachers and students will benefit from improved performance.

One problem here is that telling isn't teaching, and when everything related to these massive improvement efforts unfolds in a single morning in the hands of training personnel using lecture as the main mode of delivery, the effect is much the same as it is in classrooms where teachers lecture day after day. In my own workshops, I always ask teachers if they have attended night classes or professional-development sessions where, after fifteen minutes or so, they have gone to a better place in their minds. They always laugh, and then all those workshop participants *put their hands in the air*. They understand that we can *attend* something, while at the same time tuning out what is being said by whoever is doing the talking. It is not enough to tell teachers what needs to be done; it is far more effective to model several practical strategies with the teachers present, thus turning them from (passive) attendees into (active) participants.

If, for example, a school district has lined up behind a push to improve reading scores, and if there are several proven strategies that will help accomplish said improvement, then those strategies should be modeled in the sessions in the *exact same way* as they can and should be used in classrooms. It is much more effective and beneficial when seminars are turned into practical workshops, with workshop leaders who facilitate process and participants *who actually participate*.

If it is necessary to communicate the structure of the continuous-improvement plan, then that can be done quickly, and a website can be set up to provide additional information and updates throughout the implementation process.

Beyond the modeling that takes place in those first professional-development workshops, instructional leaders from the building and from central office should be in the classrooms modeling, observing, and working with teachers to improve instruction in that specific area. When the strategies modeled in the workshops and in the classrooms begin to show signs of success, teachers are much more likely to become believers. I have found that there is nothing more exciting than hearing a teacher describe something new that has worked for her *and* for her students. However, if all that happens in the mandatory morning seminar is that one person after another walks teachers through the master plan, there is likely to be little from those sessions that is translated into honest-to-goodness improvement.

Seeking Multiple Perspectives

When teachers work in isolation, they tend to see the world through one set of eyes—their own. The fact that there might be someone somewhere *in the same building or district* who may be more successful at teaching this or that subject or lesson is lost on teachers who close the door and work their way through the school calendar virtually alone. Schmoker (2006) laments that he and his colleagues "were kept from seeing evidence that some teachers were vastly more effective than others" (p. 27). In the absence of a process that allows them to benchmark with those who do things better or at least differently, teachers are left with that one perspective—their own. I taught various subjects under the social studies umbrella and had very little idea of how my peers who taught the same subject did what they did. The idea of meeting regularly to compare notes, plan common assessments, and share what we did well never occurred to us. Rather, we spent much time in the social studies office complaining about a lack of time . . . and playing the blame game.

Most teachers would, if given the chance and some clear direction, benefit from the perspectives of colleagues in their own buildings or districts. One of the most valuable trips I ever made with a group of administrators and teachers was to a school district about three hours from our own. It was extremely valuable to see how teachers did what they did in three different schools in that district;

the ride home made for some incredible introspection and melding of views. We had seen the same classrooms, met the same teachers, and observed the same lessons, yet we came away with different perspectives that made our conversations—and our subsequent planning—much richer.

Administrators, whether or not there is a district-wide improvement effort afoot, need to make certain that teachers get to see other teachers in action. I can't think of a better use of the substitute-teacher budget line than making it possible for teachers to leave their classrooms and get the balcony view in classrooms of the school's or district's most successful teachers. I am not saying that teachers should be encouraged to do this if only they can find the time; *I am saying that administrators should make it happen.* Observing and meeting with other teachers on a regular basis is something that should be facilitated by the building's leadership team. Time should be allowed for the observer and the observed to get together and share how the class went and how it could have been yet more effective. These postobservation conversations allow both teachers to reflect on learning and teaching in general, not just on what happened in that particular class.

Davidovich, Nikolay, Laugerman, and Commodore (2010) call this *letting ideas collide* in an atmosphere of dynamic interaction that "happens when leaders create the conditions where people can do meaningful work together. Ideas collide when teachers share their understanding, discover one another's thinking, and together develop a deeper understanding of the practices that really work for students." Released from isolation, teachers can observe other teachers and then discuss *why* what she did worked and *what effect* it had on student performance. In this case, the ideas of the observer collide with the ideas of the observed, and this collision "leads to reordering when the new understandings can openly engage existing practice" (p. 162).

The key here is that administrators and teachers concentrate on the improvement of existing practice through the kind of teacher interaction *that focuses on what is actually going on in the classroom.* Fullan (2010) correctly points out that "to get anywhere, you have to *do* something" (p. 32). The doing in this case involves leadership teams committing to faculty collaboration through observations and postobservation discussions; the teachers, for their part, can focus on instruction in a way that directly facilitates instructional improvement, along with teacher and student success. A teacher who becomes excited because something new worked, or because she observed something great in another classroom, is much more likely to travel

adopted for six or more years; the routine is reinforced one chapter or unit after another. It is this sameness that may actually prevent continuous improvement for classroom teachers and their students. In this sameness, there is comfort.

When I first started teaching, I was hired to teach history to eighth graders. What this meant to me, of course, was that my job was to present the information to my students; their job was to sit (quietly), take a few notes, and go home to process the information they had gathered in preparation for the next regularly scheduled quiz or test. My students were willing or unwilling receptacles, into which I poured a concoction composed of the events, dates, personalities, humorous anecdotes, and happenings from the history of our country. The information flow was decidedly one way—from me to them—and my idea of interaction was for me to ask questions and solicit answers from pretty much the same kids in each class—my fan club. In *A Place Called School* (1984/2004), John Goodlad and a team of researchers recorded the findings of their collective observations of hundreds of classrooms in dozens of schools. A large percentage of those classrooms apparently looked very much like my own; teachers talked, while students listened (or not). Teachers would occasionally ask a question and seek a response, but in large measure this was the extent of the interaction. Students may have responded to teachers, but "teachers were not responding to students in large part because students were not initiating anything" (p. 229). Goodlad and his team did not observe "much opportunity for students to become engaged with knowledge so as to employ their full range of intellectual abilities" (p. 231). My own observations of hundreds of classrooms over four decades have brought me to the conclusion that teachers are doing too much of the work, while students do too little.

For their part—and this is consistent with my own observations over time—the students Goodlad and his team observed were involved to the extent that they were "lectured to and working on written assignments" that were workbook- and worksheet-driven (p. 231). Students' time in school is too often spent having something done *to them*, rather than doing something that will benefit them in any meaningful way. This is not rocket science; in order to learn to communicate clearly, think critically, solve problems, and pose thoughtful questions, *students actually have to be given the time to communicate clearly, think critically, solve problems, and pose thoughtful questions.* There is no shortcut here, and classroom time must be spent wisely.

If there is anything we have learned in the information age, it is that there is no lack of information out there. One click of a mouse can bring to the screen, in full view of the average student, more information on any subject than a teacher could impart if he spent the entire year covering just that subject. In order to be able to bring some understanding to all this requires that students be able to compare, contrast, sort and analyze, synthesize, and view whatever they see and hear with a great deal of healthy skepticism. That information to which we now have immediate access changes at an ever-increasing rate. Change is certain, and change is constant.

A New Reality for the Workplace

What employers want in their new employees is also changing. When I was in college, I spent one summer working at a machine shop. My job was simple: I put holes in metal—small holes, medium holes, large holes . . . holes. I used a punch press and a drill press. I came to work on time, followed directions, and left at the end of the day. It took no time at all for the shop foreman to teach me the routine, and then I took it from there. If I ran into problems, I called the foreman and he solved it. Everyone in the shop had his or own routine, and the only time we talked with each other was during the thirty-minute lunch. Teamwork was not really needed; critical thinking was limited to learning what one needed to learn in order to avoid accidents.

That shop is gone, and almost anything that needs to be done to metal is now done by machines. The skills needed by workers today are not the same as those needed by anyone who worked in that machine shop. In the course of writing *The Global Achievement Gap* (2008), Tony Wagner interviewed the CEO of a company that supports the manufacture of microelectronic devices by way of providing chemicals and machinery. Wagner asked what the CEO looks for in new employees, and the CEO said he looked for people who know how to ask good questions and communicate clearly with teammates and customers alike (p. 2). Wagner goes on to lament the fact that current educational reform efforts "might not result in all students knowing how to ask good questions" (p. 3). Teaching students how to communicate in an articulate manner, work in teams, and ask the kinds of questions that lead to clear understanding can only be a result of changing the way we do what we do in the classroom.

Shifting the Load From Teachers to Learners

Learner-centered classrooms are those in which students carry a heavier load and in which students are part of a true learning community. According to Darling-Hammond (2008), if we want students to be able to deal with the rapid change that characterizes the twenty-first century, classrooms must be designed that "foster communities of discourse that make students' and teachers' thinking visible." Classroom environments must motivate students "by minimizing comparison, and by fostering opportunities for risk taking and improvement over time" (p. 197). A classroom where it is obvious to students that the teacher is not willing to take risks on their behalf is not likely to lead to risk taking on the part of the students themselves. If the teacher plays it safe, the students will do the same. They will sit, listen (or appear to listen), smile (or not), and "play the school game." Teachers have to change and show a willingness to foster risk taking in a classroom dedicated to continuous improvement.

I recently ran into an old friend, a biology teacher and swim coach who exudes energy, refuses to play the blame game, and consistently produces winners in his classroom and on his swim team. Joe Gentry's systems for success include processes that are constantly in line for review and refinement. Gentry's students and swim team members understand that in this teacher and coach they have someone who has their success firmly at the forefront, and when he and I ran into each other, he was poring over thirty e-mails from students who were asking about him (he was on a few days sick leave) and seeking clarification concerning assignments. Gentry's classroom clicks, and his students and teams perform. Every single one of his 138 biology students passed the state exam, and his swim teams are always in contention for local, regional, and state honors. His commitment to continuous improvement is deeply rooted in his commitment to the kids for whom he works tirelessly, year after year. He constantly takes appropriate risks on behalf of his biology students and his student swimmers, and they appreciate it . . . and him.

We as educators ought to be concerned with preparing students for their future, and there is no better way to do that than to encourage their inquisitiveness, improve their listening skills, and create a climate where they can ask questions and question what they see and hear on a regular basis. One thing is for certain: Change will continue to come quickly, and we must help students be able to deal with it and welcome it. Covington (1992) says that "change is best handled, and even welcomed, when individuals possess a well-developed arsenal of mental skills associated with original, creative, and independent thinking" (p. 3). I can't speak for other teachers, but I can say with certainty that, at least until my last couple of years of teaching, my classrooms were passive—not active—places, where I did most of the work, while my students frequently went to a better place in their minds a good deal of the time.

A teacher's continuous-improvement journey must involve her students as part of a collaborative exercise. Active and engaging classroom communities are ones in which teachers and students fully embrace risk taking and change. The best teachers I know are totally transparent in their quest for improvement. They let the kids in on it from Day 1, and everyone in those classroom communities learns, grows, and gets better together. Every teacher ought to take the time to consider where she is in terms of a willingness to change and *to acknowledge the difficulty and benefit of that change.* Teachers and administrators are, in the words of Michael Fullan (2010), "change leaders" whose goals ought to be to "get movement in an improved direction" (p. 9). Every teacher in every classroom should be all about movement in an improved direction, for herself and the students in her care. The journey itself begins with the willingness to change and a commitment to trying to determine where the baseline is along a continuum from a teacher-centered to a more learner-centered environment.

Determining Where You Are

In any journey, understanding *where you are* and *where you want to go* are both absolutely necessary. In the continuous-improvement journey, the paths may be many, but the ultimate destination keeps moving ahead of the continuous-improvement process. It is a journey without end; the beauty of the trip is that there is always room for improvement. But it all begins with an understanding of where you are on a skill-development continuum. Where the students are in terms of their own performance is also part of knowing where you are as a teacher. In fact, teachers dedicated to a continuous-improvement program will need to find multiple ways to measure progress.

Teachers who are faced with a situation—of their own making or otherwise—where working at getting demonstrably better is now at the front of the to-do list would do well to look at where they are currently. By this I don't mean where they are in terms of how comfortable they are with what they are doing, but where they are in terms of how successful they are at continually accelerating the academic and intellectual growth of students. This is the role of the teachers: to facilitate by their actions the continuous improvement of kids. This starts with improving classroom practice, and *that* begins by taking a close look at what is working well and what is not working at all. Some processes stand in need of improvement, and some processes need to be shown the door.

Teachers can—alone or with grade-level partners—look at the results of standardized tests, diagnostic tests, benchmark assessments, reading scores, writing scores, and anything else that can be measured, with the idea that where we are now is simply a baseline. It is a starting point in that part of the continuous-improvement journey. It is not good or bad, or right or wrong; it is just where we are as we prepare to move forward. Getting depressed and blaming external circumstances (the curriculum, the textbook, the administrators, the parents, and even the students) will not help, and they amount to barriers that must be removed. I cannot stress this enough, and we'll examine the damage that can be done by the blame game later on. What is critical to teachers moving forward is to do two things: (1) Determine where you and your students are and (2) understand that nothing happens unless something happens.

Actions, Interactions, and Interventions

If the writing scores of students on the seventh-grade Phoenix Team, as measured by the state writing exam in March, are not good year after year, then specific actions and interventions need to be taken by the members of that team in order to improve those scores. If those actions and interventions improve student writing skills steadily throughout the following school year, and if the scores improve in the spring, *the Phoenix Team is not done.* They need to celebrate, to be sure, and then take whatever time is necessary in order to discover and plan new actions that, along with the old, successful ones, will facilitate progress. The baseline is moved as a result not of whatever actions and interventions move it along a continuous-improvement continuum.

The sixth-grade Cardinal Team may discover, through a close examination of the available data, that those critical-thinking skills that would benefit students in every one of the subject areas are decidedly lacking. Working with building administrators, those team members can do the research into best practices that will surface ideas and interventions that will accelerate their students' growth in the area of critical thinking. Principals can clear the way for two teachers on the Cardinal Team to observe the classroom of a teacher at another middle school who has, over the years, demonstrated a remarkable ability to develop in her students a capacity for critical thinking and problem solving. The visit to that teacher's classroom can be followed up with a postobservation conference that will allow the two Cardinal Team teachers and the teacher they observed to compare notes.

Once again, it comes down to reflecting on how we can shift students along a continuous-improvement continuum, depending on (1) where each of them is currently and (2) where and how far each needs to go in the name of progress. Reflective efforts can and should involve students, as they set individual and class goals. As we'll see in Chapter 7, run charts and bar graphs can provide markers or signposts on the way to those goals, and individual conferences between the teacher and individual students can serve as improvement accelerators. Harnessing the power of reflection requires that teachers *make time* to reflect individually, collectively with peers, and in partnership with students.

Different Strokes and Different Schedules

A main focus for the seventh-grade Phoenix Team at this fictional middle school is the writing process. The sixth-grade Cardinal Team devoted a good deal of energy to moving the bar on critical-thinking skills for their students. In their school, there was no kickoff for the year of improvement at the middle school. The administration did pull together a small cadre of teachers, administrators, and others that served as a permanent process-improvement team, the purpose of which was to examine processes around the school (customer service, bus-loop safety, etc.). The team met regularly to surface issues that might require professional development or action research. Every administrator spent a good deal of time in classrooms, where the focus was on continuous improvement, even though the main area of focus, as we have seen, might be different from team to team and room to room.

The wonderful thing about being a member of a middle school team is that the team meets regularly; it is up to the administration in the building and the team members themselves to make valuable use of that planning time. Elementary teachers generally have precious little time to themselves, much less to meet with other teachers at their grade level. Rebecca DuFour (Eaker, DuFour, & DuFour, 2002), when she was an elementary principal, understood this lack of time and got creative with the scheduling in order to free up personal planning time for teachers and, importantly for her school's continuous-improvement efforts, "an hour to an hour and 10 minutes each week of uninterrupted collaborative team time" (p. 64). She did this by providing covers, and it was understood that the planning time thus created was to be used to analyze data, identify student strengths and weaknesses, and establish improvement targets (p. 65). Principals at whatever level need to take the steps necessary to provide collaborative chunks of time, and then make certain the time is used wisely. Great fanfare need not accompany school-improvement efforts, but administrators should make it clear that getting better is not an option. Improving performance will happen at different levels and in different ways for teachers and staff, but it will happen.

The Nonnegotiable Part

One of the finest principals I have ever had the pleasure of knowing has a favorite phrase, taken from Schmidt's (2002) *Gardening in the Minefield: A Survival Guide for School Administrators*. The phrase is "gentle pressure, relentlessly applied," and the application here is that continuous improvement for schools cannot be a negotiable proposition. The status quo may be comfortable for teachers and staff, but change is required in order to make a shift along the continuous-improvement continuum. A building administrator must model this by continually shifting along that line, improving her own performance and increasing her effectiveness.

    As I mentioned earlier, it is possible to restructure schedules so that teachers can have the time to determine where they and their students are, set realistic goals (and benchmarks) for improvement, implement the interventions needed to shift progress ever toward those goals, evaluate the effectiveness of the interventions, and adjust accordingly. Administrators do not have to frighten staff with the next big thing right out of the gate in August; indeed, continuous improvement is possible through the application of little things that happen all over the building—from the front office to the cafeteria to the classrooms. Individual teachers and groups of teachers, along with individuals and groups of support staff employees, can make a tremendous difference in the lives of the students in their care, but only if everyone understands that movement away from the status quo is nonnegotiable: gentle pressure, relentlessly applied.

Final Thoughts

There is a temptation on the part of districts to introduce large and complicated change mechanisms that will most certainly come into conflict with the status quo in schools and classrooms. The pain that results from these well-meaning improvement efforts can be avoided if administrators, teachers, and employees are brought into the process early on. Leadership teams can be formed and empowered to identify areas of improvement. Because they are closest to the problems, they can be part of a collaborative effort when it comes to finding solutions. Improvement can come in gradual steps and need not be trotted out with marching bands and great fanfare. Harnessing the power of reflection can lead to substantial improvement in all areas of school life, from the classroom to the cafeteria to the front office. Administrators at every level need to create an environment that is conducive to the continuous-improvement process.

In Chapter 3, we'll explore environmental factors that can serve as accelerants to school improvement.

3

School Environment as Accelerant

Over four decades in education, including nine years in educational sales and sales management, I have been in hundreds of schools, and I have found that in a very short period of time after entering the building, one can get a fairly accurate idea of how committed that school is to continuous improvement. In one school, during my years as a sales representative, I actually broke up a fight in a busy hallway. I noticed with a good deal of irritation that there were no faculty members or administrators in that hallway when the fight occurred, which was during the change of classes. It was a student who helped me separate the two combatants, and as we traveled to the office, adults were noticeably absent from the hallways through which we traveled. My experience in that school was negative, to say the very least, and the attitudes I encountered on the part of adults could not have failed to serve as a barrier to progress. My impression was that everyone was treading water, and indifference was the order of the day.

In some schools, I have encountered one or two people whose positive attitude stands out in stark contrast to others who don't seem to enjoy their jobs in the least. On the other hand, I have been in schools where I have been warmly welcomed on entering the building, and that positive greeting has been amplified in the main office and by administrators, teachers, and staff. In these schools, it is easy to imagine that forward progress is accelerated by the attitudes and efforts of adults and students alike. A trip to the school cafeteria during lunch, a visit to the restroom, a long walk through the halls, and being present when the buses arrive in the morning or leave at night—these opportunities to observe and reflect tell a visitor much about the way things are in a particular school building. Weak or seemingly nonexistent processes serve as evidence of the absence of a systemic approach to continuous improvement.

Absolutely everyone contributes in one way or another toward an environment that either encourages or discourages forward progress. Anything that is noticeable to a visitor is also in plain sight on a daily basis for regular members of the school community. In one school, I passed two custodians in a hallway; both were oblivious to the paper that was scattered about on the floor, and both were unconcerned with the coats and notebooks sticking out of several opened, partially opened, or jammed-shut-but-not-latched lockers. Indeed, much can be inferred from simply walking through a school building during the course of the school day. None of what I saw was lost on the kids who walked those same hallways; the example set for them was deplorable and unfortunate. If the adults who inhabited the building—including the custodians—did not care about what the place looked like, why should the students?

I have also been in schools where the exact opposite of what I have described was the case. I have seen elementary schools where students moved in an orderly fashion down one side of a hallway in a way that did not disturb the classrooms of teachers and students who were busy with the work at hand. I have eaten in school cafeterias where the students cleaned up after themselves *without being reminded*, much less scolded. I have seen hallways brightened by student work, and I have visited classrooms where students love where they are and what they are doing. I have been in schools where the principal will greet students in the hallway by name, and where courtesy and respect are coins of the realm. I have been in schools where the custodians kept the place spotless, from the hallways to the classrooms to the restrooms—and took great pride in doing so. When I am in a building that is clean and inviting, I make it a point to find the head custodian and let that person know what my observations say about their commitment to excellence.

It is also true that a building can be clean and the hallways quiet, while saying little about what is going on in the classrooms. The best principals whom I have had the pleasure of knowing over the years are those who, by their own example, set the tone for continuous improvement. They are out and about in their buildings, and they know the teachers and the students. They know exactly what is happening in classrooms for the simple reason that they spend a good deal of time there. They are positive professionals who understand that a truly effective continuous-improvement effort is one that has no end. For everyone in those kinds of positive and forward-looking environments, continually making progress in a hundred different important areas is not optional. Improvement from one corner of the school to another is nonnegotiable.

Awareness and Progress as Twin Norms

Great principals understand that every facet of every single thing that goes on in the school community is capable of being improved. Those principals know that there is not a process or program in sight that cannot be made better. The great heart of a building lies in its classrooms, and great principals are always in those classrooms. They are not "snoopervising" during those visits; they are looking for ways to help teachers get better at what they do. Highly successful school leaders utilize formative evaluation processes that allow teachers to take risks, make adjustments, and move forward in their own continuous-improvement journeys. Also, great principals know it is not enough that the hallways are clean of litter (although they are) or that students behave when walking from classroom to classroom (although they do) or that mutual respect is the order of the day every day (although it is); those administrators help accelerate learning in the classroom by providing gobs of meaningful and timely feedback and by providing a safe and supportive environment.

Schmoker (2006) gives us a compelling reason why our nation's schools are not more successful. It is because "the most important people within and outside schools know very little about what actually goes on inside them" (p. 13). In many cases, if things *seem* to be going well, they must be going well. However, the best principals at every level are not even remotely satisfied with the way things *seem*. They *know* exactly what is going on in the building's classrooms, *for the simple reason that they are in there frequently.* Schmoker suggests that both teachers and administrators tour classrooms, not in a search for perfection but "for schoolwide patterns with respect to two things:

1. the general quality and substance of instruction

2. students' attentiveness—are most of them "on task?" (p. 15)

Teachers can learn much from getting "the balcony view" in classrooms other than their own. Relieved of the normal duties associated with running their own classrooms for an hour or two, teachers can observe and consider what they see in relation to Schmoker's two points: quality and student attentiveness.

With an eye toward quality and student engagement, every classroom process can be improved; every student can make progress; every teacher can operate more effectively next week than she did this week. The job of the principal and the building's leadership team is to make it clear that (1) improvement is not an option and that (2) the support will be there for that improvement effort. The principal who makes it clear that everyone in the building—from the front office to the classroom—will be involved in the improvement effort is *not* saying that we are operating from a standpoint of deficiency. This needs to be made clear from the start. There is no one in the school community, including the principal, who is not capable of improving the processes that make progress possible. Where we are in our development as professionals is simply where we are; it is a convenient baseline, and our job is to make steady progress down the continuous-improvement highway.

Great administrators and other building-level supervisors are not content with observing teachers and other employees as they work. They hold reflective conversations with individuals and groups in an attempt to surface systems that are broken or processes in need of improvement; they assemble improvement teams in order to adjust or replace ineffective processes. They make it known that baselines are *starting points* for making things better, and where we are is simply a way station on the way to where we are going. Importantly, great administrators do not play the blame game in the faculty lounge, at a party, or anywhere else.

Avoiding the Blame Game

When I started teaching, we teachers would sit around the faculty lounge bemoaning the fact that we did not have time to do what we needed to do. The delicious irony involved in taking huge chunks of time complaining about the lack of time eluded us, as I look back on it. When test results were poor, or when students were not performing up to expectations, we managed to find a veritable plethora of causes: the curriculum was too extensive, the textbooks were unreadable, the parents were unsupportive, and the students—well, the students were not what they used to be, whatever that was, in our day. I can't remember an occasion when someone said, "You know, I hate to admit this, but maybe we need to improve our instruction." That insolence would have been met, no doubt, with stony silence, followed by a long and verbal list of things beyond our control that held us back.

Jenkins (2003) puts it well when he says, "If blame could improve schooling, American K–12 education would be the envy of the world" (p. xxv). In fact, according to Jenkins, playing the blame game does not fix anything; it permits those in charge to escape responsibility; and it keeps us from searching further for the root causes (p. xxvi). An environment in which the blame game is played constantly will serve as a powerful impediment to improvement. Principals must make it clear that blaming everyone and everything else is both counterproductive and unacceptable. Problems deserve solutions, not scapegoats. Any program of continuous improvement will wither in the face of the blame game. I know principals who deal with this directly and effectively when it arises, so that it cannot infect the positive, forward-looking environment they are working so hard to create and maintain.

Knowing that the blame game can be an impediment to progress presents administrators and leadership teams with another opportunity to harness the power of reflection. A representative group of teachers and other school employees can be brought together to brainstorm ways in which the blame game affects the continuous-improvement process, and that same group can work on ways to keep it from happening. What may be most effective is a principal who says, "We don't play the blame game here," and backs that up in conferences with teachers who continue to do it. Administrators who do not themselves play the blame game are in a much better position to eradicate its use in the building.

The Committee Word

In my years as a teacher, I was assigned to a good many committees formed with the best of intentions—to implement change and improve working conditions, safety, communication, and instruction. If there were several meetings during the school year, attendance at each successive meeting dwindled. On more than one occasion, I can remember one of my colleagues glancing at her watch, rolling her eyes, and announcing without much enthusiasm that she had to get to a committee meeting. As I recall, our expectations concerning those committees and those meetings were rather low, and the impact of such efforts at improvement was slight.

One reason I think many people (I include myself here) hate committee meetings has to do with what often happens:

- The meetings start late, in some cases because those ostensibly running them arrive late.
- They proceed in an unfocused manner, with side conversations and frequent interruptions.
- One person is permitted to vent or ramble on for large blocks of time.
- Little is actually accomplished, and virtually nothing may be decided.
- Few, if any, committee members really understand why they are there in the first place.

I would begin any attempt to get school employees involved in an ongoing improvement effort by abolishing the word committee. Take it out of the lexicon, have it removed from the subconscious, and fine anyone who uses the word (hyperbolically speaking, of course). The connotation of that word is such that it sends shivers up and down the spines of those who are *chosen* as members of the committee. Schmidt (2002) says, "Committee is a leaden word. It has the taint of showing up and sticking it out as the main criteria for success" (p. 72). Too many employees have been to too many committee meetings where little was accomplished, many were blamed, and the lack of focus was both apparent and annoying. Too many meetings have resulted in little in the way of follow-up, and nothing in the way of concrete, measurable results. Few school employees are in a rush to volunteer for committees of any sort. I was once in a school where the principal solved this by simply appointing everyone in the building at random to one of seven or eight committees.

The reason there may be a lack of focus in meetings is that there is a clear lack of purpose and direction from the start. Busy people involved in meetings need to understand from the start exactly what it is the group is intended to accomplish. Have they been pulled together simply to offer up some ideas about a specific topic? Will we simply give feedback on a given topic, after which the appropriate administrator will make the final decision? Are we here to make a decision? These are important questions that must be answered. On too many occasions, school employees who thought they were there to make a decision found out later on that nothing they thought they had decided found its way into the final product or outcome. When members of a committee feel uncomfortable or unfulfilled after leaving the building, *the real meeting will take place in the parking lot.* If committee members feel undervalued, or if they feel they were not able to say what was on their minds, they will unburden themselves to others later on, and this has an inhibitive effect on any overall improvement effort.

If this is the Beautification Committee on which we find ourselves, is the committee chair looking for ways to spruce up the building? If so, then this needs to be made clear. It is possible that there is simply $1,500 in the School Beautification fund, and administrators are seeking ways to spend it. If that is the case, the meeting can be blessedly short, money can be allocated, and everyone can go home. But, if those on the committee thought from the beginning that they were part of some grand school-climate improvement effort, and they were never disabused of that notion, their dissatisfaction will become a negative drag on the school environment by adding to the level of cynicism in the building.

In addition to knowing exactly what is expected of them as members of a group of employees charged with a specific task, those involved want to know there is someone to facilitate process during the meetings. School districts can help here by offering training for process facilitators out of the central office. These could be employees who are trained in the art of turning a group into a team and making sure a set of operational norms is adhered to during each meeting. These facilitators can ensure that time limits are honored, and they can make certain different perspectives are heard, even from those normally reluctant to share. Process facilitators are valuable people, and a good facilitator can ensure that progress is made, benchmarks are met, and a final product is forthcoming.

Project Thinking

Instead of creating committees, each of which might handle a range of school-based needs throughout the year, Schmidt (2002) suggests that teams be formed based on projects that need to be done in the school. The team is responsible for getting the job done, reporting to faculty as needed, and its members, according to Schmidt, should "use the whole group as a resource for input, brainstorming, feedback, and refinements" (p. 72). The project team is together until the job is done, at which point it is dissolved. An example might be a project team that is called together to take care of beautification efforts on the external grounds of the school and in the courtyards. This project would certainly be part of an overall customer-service commitment as it relates to first impressions for visitors, and the creation of a beautiful physical environment for students and adults alike.

The timely and successful completion of several projects by teams specifically chosen to deal with those projects can make believers out of skeptics, and participants out of cynics. The key here is that the teams must work steadily toward the established goal. Getting things done, and done well, is its own reward. Administrators should be quick to thank these teams along the way, and one last time after the successful completion of the project. The word committee need never be mentioned.

Discussion to Dialogue

I have found that if a meeting is moving along quickly, everyone seems to be in agreement, and the solution to whatever problem is being tackled seems near, then *something is decidedly wrong with the process.* If whoever is in charge is not asking for input from the silent members, and is allowing too much input from the extroverts in the group, then whoever is running the meeting *is not actually running the meeting.* Those who are silent in the meeting room will unload in the parking lot or over the phone that evening, and some ideas or concerns that should have been surfaced when they could do some good are simply wasted. Good leaders solicit the opinions, ideas, and feedback from everyone in the room, as well as from everyone in the organization. Teams also need to take the time to reflect on the difference between discussion and dialogue.

Costa (2008) defines meeting discussions this way: "During discussion, individuals offer data, knowledge, their ideas, information, rationales for positions on issues, and frequently try to convince others to take on their position." However, as we all know, discussions can deteriorate as those ideas (and personalities) come into conflict, at which point, according to Costa, "members talk past one another and little understanding occurs" (p. 143). "At its most ineffective," according to Garmston and Wellman (1999), "discussion is a hurling of ideas at one another" (p. 57). My experience is that when the ideas are flying around the meeting room, some group members duck, while others catch the ideas and hurl them back, while still others simply go to a better place in their minds. When the veneer of amicability present at the first of several meetings breaks down in the face of strong feelings and closely held beliefs, the result can be disastrous. I have seen groups simply dissolve when this happens.

When progress needs to be made, things need to get done, and goals need to be met, dialogue can replace discussion. Garmston and Wellman (1999) describe dialogue as "a reflective learning process in which group members seek to understand each other's viewpoints and deeply held assumptions" (p. 55). Costa (2008) adds that "dialogues have the primary intent of expanding the permutations and possibilities of the ideas, knowledge, and issues in order to discover new solutions" (p. 143). For me, the key here is empathy, and a willingness to withhold judgment when someone else on the team presents ideas or other input that does not necessarily fit into our own worldview or current understanding of whatever was shared. "Dialogue creates an emotional and cognitive safety zone in which ideas flow for examination without judgment" (Garmston & Wellman, 1999, p. 55). If groups of employees working on solutions to problems within the building can commit to reflecting deeply on their own and others' ideas and assumptions, this may well create a permanent environment within which real progress can be made.

Opposing points of view are inevitable and serve to surface perspectives that provide rich context for the eventual innovations recommended by the team. This can create dissonance, of course, but this is not to be avoided. In the continuous-improvement process, dissonance is not only desired—it should be welcomed. Getting along is not the goal; deciding on the best, and ultimately the most effective, course of action is the goal. Dissonance on a team creates discomfort, yet it is outside our comfort zones that we learn and grow. Davidovich et al. (2010) advise us to deal with this dissonance by saying, "'It's not about me'": "This little statement can help you move your awareness from an egocentric position to one of being part of something larger" (p. 113). This is difficult for team members; it is, however, one more opportunity for collective reflection on the part of the team. Before the team tackles the project or process that brought it together, it is critical that the team leader or a process facilitator, if one is available, help the team deal directly with the issues of discussion, dialogue, and dissonance. Surfacing and dealing with these potential pitfalls right up front may well make the difference between success and failure for the team. Done effectively, it also provides a model for other teams, as they seek to make progress along the continuous-improvement continuum.

The Going Gets Tough

When employees are brought together in order to identify and remove barriers to progress, or to solve problems of long standing, the work will be difficult. The administrators who are responsible for assembling the groups, turning them into teams, and making sure whatever gets decided is implemented need to understand that true progress on the continuous-improvement highway is going to mean long hours, various levels of conflict, and a need for everyone involved to commit to the long haul. Reeves (2009) reminds us that true collaboration involves heavy lifting, and those driving the collaborative effort cannot be doing so in a search for popularity: "If your true goal is popularity, then you are finished, and professional collaboration will meet the same fate as every other change that failed because the true standard was popularity, rather than effectiveness" (p. 48). I know highly successful principals who are effective as change agents because their standard is what works, rather than what makes them look good or makes everyone else feel good in the short term.

Even the most powerful cynics *may* well get on board eventually, if what is being implemented is working to the benefit of the organization. What made many of them cynics in the first place was being handed too many binders that tab-indexed the next big thing that was being rolled out to great fanfare. Real movement on the continuous-improvement highway happens not in the planning stage but in the implementation phase. If improvement teams spend too many meetings doing too much planning, making the binder expand by the month, *without doing something to see how it works*, people can get discouraged. Fullan (2010) says we ought not to do away with the planning phase, "but get to action sooner, and treat it as a learning period" (p. 24). One Canadian district, reports Fullan, reduced the page count in their yearly plans from forty-five to twenty-two to eight over three years, beginning in 2007. Reeves (2009) reports an Illinois district that showed significant academic gains over five years while working off of a one-page plan (p. 83). It is not the number of pages or the size of the plan that results in success; it is the commitment of those involved to move from planning to action that gets things done.

It could be said that any school working on continuous improvement is always in the planning stages, if that includes implementing changes that can then be monitored and assessed for their effectiveness. For example, a group of four grade-level teachers that meets twice per week for forty-five minutes may always be said to be in a permanent state of planning and implementation as the teacher members try things in their classrooms, assess their effectiveness, make adjustments, and insert what works into their future plans.

The key here—and this is true at any level (classrooms, schools, districts)—is that the implementation ball must be in play continually, as teachers, administrators, supervisors, classified employees, and students *plan something, try it out, assess its effectiveness, make adjustments*, and then implement the improved process at a later date. Building leaders need to be willing to constantly experiment and, by so doing, encourage employees to do the same. A dynamic school is one that is in a constant state of flux, trying this, evaluating that, making adjustments, and continually taking appropriate risks on behalf of kids. I encourage teachers to experiment constantly—at some point we simply need to *try things*.

Get Past *Planning* to Try Things and Just Try Things

I sometimes think we plan things to death. We expend so much kinetic energy in creating the grand plan that we have little energy left to implement the plan. Or, the plan we create is, on occasion, so massive in scope that no one in the organization really understands it. Or, the plan that is created is well crafted and covers all the bases but is not anywhere in evidence in the organization. One reason for the failure of a plan to result in implementation may be in the rigidity of the implementation phase; if the plan contains the answers to what ails the system, and if changes in practice are limited to those set answers, then this has the unhappy effect of discouraging teachers from asking their own questions and seeking their own solutions.

For example, a curriculum that is overly prescriptive and takes a one-size-fits-all approach to improvement makes teachers rely on those who created the curriculum for answers; it may also not allow for the time teachers need to experiment on their own, with ideas outside the confines of the set piece and largely prescriptive curriculum. It also gives teachers the chance to blame the curriculum if its implementation is not successful. Teachers and employees need to be empowered to make changes on their own, experimenting and taking the kinds of risks that will succeed (or not) and help them to build their own capacity for self-renewal and continuous improvement.

In *Change by Design: How Design Thinking Transforms Organizations and Inspires Innovation* (2009), Tim Brown argues that successful organizations need to encourage an attitude of experimentation and a culture of optimism, among other things, as a way to improve the organization and get the job done, whatever the job may be. Brown is talking about design thinking here, and so am I. As teachers go about the business of designing classrooms that are safe, positive, and challenging places where students can feel free to take risks on their own continuous-improvement journeys, building leaders need to create an optimistic culture that allows and encourages experimentation.

In order to encourage experimentation, it is not enough for administrators to *be* optimistic; the *culture* of optimism that Brown advocates must be part of the fabric of the school community. A culture of pessimism inhibits progress; a culture of optimism is an accelerant to improvement. The blame game must be sent packing, and teachers and staff must learn that risk taking in the name of continuous improvement is expected. An optimistic approach to how we are doing what we are doing in the building and in the classroom should be both modeled and mandatory. Brown (2009) puts it this way: "Without optimism—the unshakable belief that things could be better than they are—the will to experiment will be continuously frustrated until it withers" (p. 76). Schools dedicated to continuous improvement are places where employees feel empowered to take risks on behalf of kids.

Over four decades in education, I have heard teachers—frustrated because they work in an environment that is not conducive to risk taking or mistake making—say (either *sotto voce* or out loud to building leaders), "Just tell me what you want me to do!" In this short, meaning-laden exclamation is often the disappointing and de-motivating realization that experimentation is frowned upon, and playing conservative, safe cards is what is expected. New and veteran teachers who are otherwise willing to take chances and experiment on behalf of students must feel free to do so. With that empowerment, of course, goes the responsibility of experimenting in an appropriate manner.

If and when teachers take those risks and make those changes, they need to evaluate the results in light of the standards set by the district and the state. The taking of responsible risks means that the accepted standards are part of the process. Whatever innovations and changes are put in place should all be connected to whatever standards exist at the state and local levels. Changes can be productive and effective in terms of outcomes, or changes can result in little or no progress. This is why evaluation is so critical; teachers need to hold every process up to the light and examine it closely. Did the implementation I just tried work? If not, what might have made it more successful? Have others tried this, and what did they find? Experimentation often leads to even more experimentation, and this builds both confidence and competence over time for teachers and employees.

On the other hand, teachers and employees who discover that making mistakes and taking risks will automatically incur the wrath of someone on the leadership team are less likely to experiment in the future. A negative culture that discourages innovation is likely to put barriers on the road in front of employees and students alike. If a teacher who wants to try things and make substantive changes finds she cannot do so, she may well ask for a transfer at the earliest opportunity. A lack of visible and ongoing support may well keep teachers who might otherwise be willing to experiment with ideas new to them from taking the risks necessary to break the power of the status quo.

In many schools, I have found that even though direct support may not be forthcoming, teachers may be left to try things out and to innovate within their own classrooms. It may also be possible to connect with other teachers in an effort to compare and contrast ideas and processes on the way to improving teacher performance and academic results for students. In this way—individually or with a small group of like-minded teachers or employees—productive change can be forthcoming. School employees willing to collaborate, take risks, and experiment can make a difference in the lives of the customers they serve.

Beyond Job Descriptions

One of the basic tenets of the Ritz Carlton Hotel customer-service system is that employees are empowered to step outside their own specifically defined duties to help customers when necessary. This goes a long way toward building a solid customer-friendly reputation for the Ritz Carlton Hotel chain. As schools work toward building a solid customer-friendly relationship with members of the neighborhood and business community most closely connected to them, instructing staff to look for serendipitous opportunities to serve visitors and students is a great asset.

In the course of a recent Virginia winter, I visited Montclair Elementary School in Prince William County, Virginia. Because of an overnight snowfall, the school was on a two-hour late start, and I was in the front hallway when the students entered the building that morning. In front of me, and directly in the path of the oncoming rush of elementary students, was a woman who was greeting the students as they entered, many of them by name. Her warm welcome was infectious, and the kids returned her smiles with grins and high fives. They all knew her, but I did not; it was only later I discovered that Julie Silverman *is the school's bookkeeper.* I suspect that one could search her job description closely, without finding "greet the kids each morning and say goodbye each afternoon in a way that makes them feel special," but that is exactly what she does at Montclair each day. Her principal, Tawnya Soltis, speaks highly of Julie, noting her "love and care for children" and her eminently positive nature, along with her "willingness to do whatever" for the school and the children who come through those front double doors every day (personal communication, July 28, 2010).

I once knew a head custodian who stood in front of the school every day, waving to passing drivers. He was a great ambassador for that school, and his retirement was a great loss for the school and, I suspect, for people like me who loved returning his smile and wave each day. A parent once told me that her daughter's favorite middle school adult was a wonderful cafeteria lady who greeted everyone by name and who always had a smile and something positive to say. Her daughter moved on to high school, but she frequently returned to her old middle school to say hello to this special member of the support staff who understood that her job was not simply to collect lunch money from kids. I taught with a teacher who regularly visited the homes of her students because she knew the importance of meeting and getting to know those parents and guardians. These actions represent value added to students and parents. In Appendix D, the reader will meet a teacher who arranged to conduct book clubs *one Saturday a month* at the home of a different student on each occasion. On *Saturday*! There were no grades assigned, but thirty-six out of her forty-one students made the effort and benefitted from the results. All these examples involve teachers who were willing to color outside the lines.

Every school district ought to encourage its employees—teachers, administrators, and support personnel—to step outside their narrow job descriptions when the opportunity arises to build appropriate relationships, accelerate student performance, help visitors, and assist peers in the building on a regular basis. Every one of these sometimes individual acts helps create and maintain the kind of positive environment within which all efforts at continuous improvement can thrive. School environments that are negative and filled with people who won't go the extra mile because "it's not my job" are barriers to any continuous-improvement effort launched by the school's leadership team. While serious improvement efforts are not merely composed of what may *seem* to some to be random acts of kindness, those positive acts cannot help but accelerate larger and more systemic improvement initiatives.

The building principal is the person to whom everyone looks for leadership, and if the principal wants to create a positive environment, then the principal needs to be seen to be positive. She cannot decree that everyone display a positive attitude at all times and then sit in the faculty lounge and leak sarcasm. The principal cannot dictate that employees go the extra mile and then hide in her office. In a business that depends on building relationships, the principal must be the chief relationship builder. When it comes to creating and maintaining an environment that accelerates the improvement process, the principal must demonstrate the energy she expects from everyone else in the school community. Those who go the extra mile must know they are appreciated.

Final Thoughts

Creating an environment that will sustain continuous-improvement efforts in the building involves more than just planning; it requires individual and collective experimentation from the front office to the classrooms to the cafeteria. A grade-level team at the elementary level whose members work together on a regular basis—implementing ideas, evaluating them, and making adjustments—can be a model for improvement. Having the most wonderful volunteer from the community at large greet visitors at the front door every day, and interact wonderfully with staff and students, will help create the kind of environment that encourages others to act in the same manner.

Principals who honor continuous-improvement planning groups by conducting focused meetings where reflective dialogue replaces dysfunctional discussion are assisting in the creation of an environment that accelerates progress. Principals who will not permit employees to play the blame game, and who refuse to play it themselves, are removing impediments to improvement that can deep-six reform efforts in any organization. Principals and their leadership teams—and there can be no exceptions—must walk the walk of improvement.

In Chapter 4, we'll shift from the building in general to the classroom in particular as we continue searching for ways to create an environment conducive to continuous improvement.

4

Classroom Environment
as Accelerant

I t is easier to get Eddie to do something Eddie actually *wants to do.*
It is also easier to enlist Eddie in his own continuous-improvement
effort if he can identify progress in terms of his own development. If
it is clear to Eddie that he can actually do something today he could
not do yesterday, he may commit himself to the continuous-
improvement journey. One small success may lead to another
successful effort, and success does feel good; there is little more
satisfying to a teacher than to see a student's eyes light up when he
gets it or otherwise demonstrates true understanding.

On the other hand, if Eddie spends most of his time watching his
teachers work, while he does little or nothing except listen, write
down a few notes, and then take quiz after quiz and test after
summative test, the truth is that he may feel disconnected from his
own educational process. As this disconnect becomes more apparent
to him over time, he is much more likely to become discouraged and,
perhaps, drop out of school.

It is the responsibility of Eddie's teachers to create a classroom
environment where he and his classmates are expected to produce,
perform, and make progress in clearly defined content and skill areas.
If telling is not really teaching, if lecture and other forms of teacher
talk limit the opportunities for students to *learn by doing*, then a larger
proportion of classroom time must be spent getting students engaged

in their own learning. No basketball coach at any level ever lectured his way to Friday night's game. The players must do the lion's share of the work, and it is the job of the coach to create the right *environment* for his team to produce, perform, and make progress from day to day and week to week during the season. This involves watching the *players* work, while providing feedback that is both timely and meaningful.

When assigning homework, quality should not be sacrificed on the altar of quantity, and teacher feedback for skill-based assignments should be corrective in nature, timely, and tied to specific criterion (Marzano, Pickering, & Pollock, 2001). In this way, students understand where they stand not relative to other students (norm referencing) but "relative to a specific target of knowledge or skill" (p. 98). Vatterott (2009) adds, "Students should have no trouble connecting homework to classroom learning" (p. 101). Students have to involve themselves in assignments with the clear understanding that meaningful feedback will be forthcoming and what they are doing with those assignments relates to what they are currently doing in that teacher's classroom.

Teachers at any grade level need to engage students in meaningful work that is enhanced and improved by feedback that informs teachers and students as they travel along the continuous-improvement highway. I often hear teachers say that kids today don't want to learn, or words to that effect. The truth is that students do *want* to learn and they *do* learn; what they don't want to do is come to school to watch *teachers* do all the work. I learned to write by writing; I learned to read by reading—and my best teachers had a way of making me *want* to do those things. By reading to me and suggesting things I might read, those teachers opened the doors for and to my imagination. My natural curiosity took over from there. Fifty years later, I can say with certainty that Eddie and all his friends each possess a rich imagination and a natural sense of wonder and curiosity that teachers can tap into in order to enhance learning and accelerate intellectual growth.

The Personal Nature of Powerful Learning

Deci (1995) reminds us of what we already know, that "for young children, learning is a primary occupation; it is what they do naturally and with considerable intensity" (p. 19). There is, with children, a natural curiosity that—when fed by adults—leads to considerable learning that has nothing whatever to do with extrinsic rewards like grades or pats on the back. When those young students are investigating, questioning (as only a young child can do!), and naturally seeking to understand the world around them, the motivation is internal; it happens as they add to their own knowledge and understanding of their environment. When kids investigate, ponder, deliberate, wonder, and question, *they are doing the work.* Questioning is natural, and it happens when a child (or anyone, for that matter) truly wants to understand something that seems puzzling or incomplete.

As students work their way through the grades in school, my experience is that teachers do more and more of the work. Teachers do more of the talking, more of the questioning (as they seek "correct" answers with closed questions), and more of the *doing.* The flow of information no longer goes in two directions; it emanates from the teacher and flows to the students. Teachers will, for example, display a picture or graph on the screen and then proceed to explain to the students exactly what it is or what it means. The students no longer have to wonder, investigate, deliberate, or even question what they see—all is revealed as the teacher *informs* students rather than asks them what they see. Relieved of any reason to think in any *active sense*, students become passive observers in a teacher-centered environment, and the workload is shifted increasingly from the students to the teachers through the grades. Teachers get a real workout in the comprehension level of the cognitive ladder when they do the explaining and describing, while students sit passively and, perhaps, go to a better place in their minds.

All human beings have a natural curiosity and a basic need to understand the world around them. Teachers can take advantage of this by, for example, showing students an image on the screen, letting them digest it for thirty seconds or so, and then having them stand and meet in a trio or quartet to ponder out loud *what it is they are looking at on the screen.* While each small group works on this, the teacher can walk around the classroom, listening to the conversations. When she hears something she would like everyone to know, she can simply ask that group if one of them would mind sharing that particular thought with everyone when they debrief. If someone in the group agrees to share, the teacher can simply call on that person later—once everyone is seated again—in order to begin a class discussion that incorporates what was discussed in the groups. By choosing two or three students to share (and getting their agreement to do so), it guarantees that critical points become part of the discussion. What gets shared as a result of what the teacher overheard as students talked in pairs or groups can become the springboard for a larger classroom conversation.

In this case, it does not matter that everyone does not know what the image is, or what it represents. The image, if it lives within the context of what the students have been covering for a day or two, will give up its secrets to some in the room; others may be content to know that *not knowing* is perfectly okay. The message is that students can learn to live with ambiguity. The students' natural curiosity about the image's purpose or identity is fed by the teacher's refusal to tell them what they are looking at on the screen. Over the years, I have seen great teachers tap their students' natural wonder and curiosity in a way that involves them in their own learning. It is powerful; it is even more powerful as students talk together in trios or quartets in order to make some sense out of the picture, graphic image, or story.

The Larger Classroom

We live in an age when academic assignments for students can harness their natural tendency to navigate the Internet in search of stories, images, and information on anything imaginable. A modern student's curiosity is unfettered by the unavailability of print resources that may have been a barrier to satisfying that curiosity in the Industrial Age. One request on Google or any other search engine can bring more hits than any student could seriously consider combing through; suffice it to say that lack of information is not a problem today. Access is instantaneous, and teachers can take advantage of the Net Generation's facility with everything electronic when assigning homework or semester- or year-long assignments. Computer availability is not limited to the home or school; the computer stations in public libraries continue to be widely used.

The Net Generation, however, does not really need buildings or stations or even classrooms to communicate and collaborate. Today, Boomers struggle with the new technology and turn to younger generations for advice. Net Gen kids grew up with this amazing electronic technology, viewing it "as just another part of their environment" according to Tapscott (2009); indeed, "for many kids, using the new technology is as natural as breathing" (p. 18). Walking along any busy street, it is common to see hand-held devices in almost constant use, allowing those familiar with them to communicate with friends, search the Internet, or watch a movie—all without the benefit of a chair, desk, or TV screen. They are engaged and they are involved, and they control the extent to which they are both. They are in charge.

Then, they walk into a high school classroom and they relinquish control to a teacher who may choose to talk for the better part of an hour. To kids who are used to images on a screen that change at the speed of click, having to watch the teacher work is—not to put too fine a point on it—less than satisfying. The engagement and involvement are gone in the sense that they have come to understand it; boredom and acting out may be the result. Teachers need to engage and involve students from the moment they enter the room. Students prefer the active to the passive; they want to be engaged in a way that they can have some aspect of control in what they do during the school day. Getting students engaged involves getting them up, moving, talking, asking questions, analyzing, inferring, defending a point of view, and otherwise getting a complete workout on the cognitive ladder. Students cannot sit on the sidelines and still be involved; teachers need to plan carefully so that students are in the game when they are in the classroom.

Teachers can involve students in every facet of skill development. Students can, for example, be involved in the creation of a checklist related to what makes a good listener. My experience is that in a structured brainstorming session, students of almost any age will surface the key components to active listening (eye contact, body language, facial expressions, asking questions, and paraphrasing in order to understand). In other words, teachers do not have to *tell* students what makes a good listener (or a good team player); they simply have to facilitate the construction of a set of principles that can lead future paired discussions or collaborative student work. I have observed teachers who have students regularly revisit the rules of good listening or collaboration, and this engages students throughout the process. Students surface key principles, help arrange them in logical order, and use them on a regular basis to guide their work with other students; the teacher's job here is to facilitate process in the interest of a smooth-running, learner-centered classroom.

Ramping Up Engagement

Teachers, then, need to shift the workload from themselves to their students. It is by doing something that we learn best, and students, according to Marzano (2003b), should be provided "with tasks and activities that are inherently engaging" (p. 149). The best way to ramp up that engagement is to give students the chance to involve themselves in their areas of interest. The speed with which students improve depends to a great extent on whether or not they are motivated to travel with confidence and agility down their own continuous-improvement highways. Trilling and Fadel (2009) put this well: "When people have an emotional connection to what is being learned—a personal experience or question—learning can be sustained longer, understanding can become deeper, and what is learned can be retained longer" (p. 33). It is simply easier to get Eddie to do something to which he is attached emotionally, or at least for which he shows some interest or curiosity.

In elementary school, I had two teachers who understood clearly that I loved to read and that I really enjoyed writing for fun. They both encouraged me in this regard. One loaned me a copy of the first Hardy Boys mystery, *The Tower Treasure*. I read it and became hooked not just on that series but on mysteries in general. The gas station where my father worked was right next to the public library in our small town. The library was diagonally across the park from my elementary school, and on more days than I can remember, I went to the library, checked out one or more mysteries, sat on a stool in the office of the gas station . . . and lost myself in those stories.

Once I was well and truly hooked on that genre, those two teachers encouraged me to write my own mystery story, and—although it took us several months—my coauthor Gary and I finally had it "published" (mimeographed, for those who remember that marvelous piece of reproductive technology); we printed and sold fifty copies at the Corner Store (it was on the corner . . . never mind). This was not a class project, nor was it part of a standardized curriculum; these two teachers simply identified writing for fun as something we might enjoy doing. They helped proof the drafts, congratulated us when we were done, and put one of us on the road to becoming an author. While we received encouragement and praise from our teachers, it was the completion of the project that gave us the most satisfaction. The motivation that drove us to the book's completion (and through the writing of a second mystery) was largely internal. At a time when no one used the term, it was one big, beautiful—and extremely informative—performance task.

Here was a project, then, the successful conclusion of which was supported by our teachers and by the skill sets (grammar, writing style, story-element development) we were learning in the classroom. These teachers were special to me because *there was something in them that saw something in us*. We were not *required* to write the stories, and there was no pressure to do so, but we were driven to finish the books by the sense of satisfaction we experienced at each stage of the project. Projects like this, according to Marzano (2003b), "are intensely personal to students and commonly have to do with long-term aspirations. Allowing students to work on long-term projects of their own choosing encourages motivation" (p. 151). Teachers who wish to create a classroom environment conducive to learning need to actively seek out those things for which students show an aptitude and in which those kids show an interest.

I'm not sure how much of an innate interest I had in grammar in elementary school, but because I learned early that I loved to write, I had a reason to become proficient in the use of punctuation, sentence structure, and everything else that affected the quality of the books I coauthored at the age of twelve. Writing offered a wonderful context for learning all the other things that would help Gary and me produce something of quality. Teachers need to provide opportunities for students of any age to experience the authentic learning that comes from projects related to what they already love to do.

Gary and I were driven by our own success, meaningful feedback from our teachers, and the feeling of satisfaction that comes from a job well done. I agree with Deci (1995) that motivation is not something that is done to people; rather, it is "something that people do" (p. 21). Children and adults are intrinsically motivated, according to Deci, when we take part in activities "simply for the feelings of excitement, accomplishment, and personal satisfaction they yield" (p. 21). In the midst of all the testing that is currently sucking a good deal of the oxygen out of classrooms across the country, we will do students a disservice if we do not provide them with opportunities to pursue their own interests in long-term projects of their own choosing. Teachers should listen to students, make an effort to identify that which moves them, and act accordingly in order to capitalize on those interests. Learning is truly personal, and it is through *doing something*—and not listening to someone else talk or lecture—that we learn best.

A Safe Place to Learn

Over the years, I have observed teachers who seem to be at odds with their students, and in those cases it is difficult to imagine that the teachers spent sufficient time and effort building solid teacher-student relationships. I have seen teachers yell at students in such a way that makes a mockery of any posted list of rules that includes something about staying calm and avoiding outbursts of anger. A teacher who loses her temper with students on a regular basis is giving those students tacit permission to do the same thing. Classrooms like this are not only ineffective; they are emotionally unsafe.

When I first started teaching in the early 1970s, student misbehavior was a constant concern in the building. My daily mantra was, "If I can just keep them seated and quiet, we can all get through the day unscathed!" I lost my temper on more than one occasion in the classroom, and it never occurred to me that by doing so, I was creating an uncertain and ultimately unsafe environment.

The climate of the classroom (and the schoolhouse as a whole) is the context in which learning will or will not take place successfully. If the climate is one in which fear and ambiguity abound, teachers and students alike are headed for trouble, perhaps as early as October. Bluestein (2008) puts it this way: "We can have the latest technology, the most appropriate furnishings and supplies, and even be exceptionally skilled in presenting information, but it is our ability to connect with our kids that makes those ingredients work best" (p. 42). The most successful teachers I have known over the years understand that relationships come first. Learning, and the students themselves, depend on it.

It is not just teacher–student relationships that are critical; student-to-student relationships will play a significant role in the continuous-improvement process in any classroom. Sarcasm and bullying on the part of students will act as barriers to success and, if allowed, will contribute to the unraveling of whatever teacher–student relationships have been developed and carefully nurtured. Worse, there are teachers for whom sarcasm and bullying are part of their repertoire. The teacher who does not model what he is teaching is teaching something entirely different.

Teachers' concerns about student behavior are understandable, and an even keel is what many teachers will say they want as they move through the school year. There are things teachers can do from late summer through the first week of school that will help create an environment that will accelerate learning:

Contact Parents Early . . . and Often

Teacher–student relationships are critical to success, and beginning on the first day of school, teachers will begin to get to know their students and develop rapport that will pay off for the rest of the school year. What many teachers ignore, however, are those all-important phone calls or visits to parents as the opening act in an attempt to get their support *early*. The moment I received my student roster, I set aside time during the day and evening to call and introduce myself to parents. While I was not able to get to every parent or guardian of my 110 or so seventh graders, I probably made contact with half of them. An interesting thing happened once school began; the students (of course) discovered from their friends that I was calling home, and those who had not received calls asked when I was going to call their parents! They had heard, you see, *that the phone calls were positive in nature*. The first year I did this, I noticed that the school year got off to a much better start in terms of student behavior and cooperation.

One key to my success with this was that students realized that I would not hesitate to call their parents. I would follow up frequently with calls that let the parents in on great things the kids had done in class or in school. All this paved the way for the other phone calls, the ones teachers *don't* like to make. When I had to make those calls, the parent(s) and I had already built a relationship. Making positive calls or visits is like putting money in the relationship bank, *against the day when a teacher has to make a withdrawal*. Those sometimes uncomfortable phone calls or person-to-person conversations were made easier for me and for the parents of my students for the simple reason that I was willing to invest in calls and visits before I even met their kids.

In doing the groundwork for *Becoming a Win-Win Teacher: Survival Strategies for the Beginning Educator*, Jane Bluestein (2010) heard from teachers who wished they had received more training in the area of building teacher–parent relationships. One teacher lamented the fact that she did not get the support she had expected to receive (p. 141). Making those early contacts may give teachers a better idea of exactly how much support they can expect during the school year. Bluestein goes on to give a critical piece of advice: "While you never want to promise something you can't or won't deliver, commit to reasonable, win-win solutions and do your best to end every contact on a positive note" (p. 148). It is a whole lot easier for teachers to be positive with parents in November if relationship building was part of August's planning.

Students are nothing if not perceptive. They watch teachers from Day 1, and they learn much as they analyze what they observe. They sit at lunch and talk with their classmates about this or that teacher. As a teacher in junior high school, I once had lunch duty three out of four lunch bells, and I can say with utter certainty that students spend at least some time during that half hour or so comparing notes on their teachers. They know, for example, after a few weeks if a teacher is likely to call home frequently, on occasion, or not at all. An excellent veteran teacher once gave me good advice: Call home beginning in August, and continue to make phone calls of support and encouragement, or just to chat a bit with parents. I took it to heart and saw a big difference in student behavior and in my own confidence as it related to dealing with the parents and guardians of my seventh graders. Students who know for certain that teachers will not hesitate to call home and build relationships with parents will factor this into their deportment, and they may work harder knowing the teacher has invested in building rapport at home.

Pay Attention to Student-to-Student Relationships

The environments in effective, learning-centered classrooms are conducive to the development of positive student-to-student relationships. Teachers who take the time to build teacher–student relationships are modeling for their students the kind of rapport building they want those students to mimic. If students are to collaborate with their peers in pairs and groups, they must develop and maintain the kind of positive, cooperative relationships that make those collaborative efforts possible. Teachers who make a conscious effort to build student-to-student relationships must spend time looking at their own normal actions and behaviors.

Over the years, I have been in classrooms where students show scant respect for the teacher and even less for their peers. In this environment, much less progress is going to be made than in a classroom where teachers spend a good deal of time developing relationships all around. In chaotic classrooms, teachers lose their cool frequently, and students follow suit. Teachers who yell in the classroom are sending a clear message: The way we get things done in here is to yell. It also puts kids in control of the classroom, and not in a productive way. Jones (2007) reminds us that when classroom teachers scold and shout, they shift control to the kids: "As the saying goes," according to Jones, "'My life is in the hands of any fool who can make me angry'" (p. 180). No one—teacher or student—is going to make much progress along the continuous-improvement highway if the classroom environment is one where chaos is a constant.

Teacher behavior is bound to affect student behavior. Teachers who consistently behave appropriately in class (do not use sarcasm, are themselves on time for class, do not verbally abuse students) are much more likely to develop the kind of collaborative environment necessary for the forward progress they seek, on the part of themselves and their students. Marzano (2003a) cites a study of college students that the opposite is true: "If [students] feel that teachers are behaving inappropriately, they will resist efforts to monitor their behavior" (p. 33). It is reasonable to assume, according to Marzano, that if this is true of college students, the study's findings "would generalize to at least high school students" (p. 33). Four decades in education make me comfortable in the assumption that elementary or middle school teachers can affect levels of student behavior and cooperation with their *own* behavior—positive and constructive, or negative and, ultimately, destructive.

Any teacher who neglects the relationships between and among students is asking for trouble. The most effective teachers I know harness the power of positive thinking, and they work every day at building rapport at the student-to-student level. They also model relationship building with students, parents, and other adults in the building. Continuous improvement in building solid relationships is accelerated when administrators, teachers, and members of the support staff create a climate of trust and safety, while modeling positive actions and behavior in the school community. Add to this a strong, mutual school–home support structure, and the classroom teacher's job just got easier.

Model Listening Skills

In my workshops, I invariably ask these two questions:

1. "How many of you had a speech course in college?" (Most of the hands go up.)

2. "How many of you had a *listening* course in college?" (One or two hands go up.)

There is no doubt that being able to speak in an articulate and confident manner is important to communicating with others face-to-face. However, at least two people are involved in any conversation, and *both* have responsibilities. While it is the responsibility of the speaker to be as clear and articulate as possible, *the listener must actively seek to understand what is being said.* That makes listening an important skill in any classroom where teachers want students to communicate in pairs, trios, or larger groups.

As important as listening is, according to Costa (2008), "it is one of the least taught skills in schools. We often say we are listening, but in actuality we are rehearsing in our head what we are going to say next when our partner is finished" (p. 33). A student who understands that his role in a pair is to listen may *look* at his partner, smile, and go to a better place in his mind. When this happens, communication breaks down. Collaborating with others, either in pairs or groups, requires that we truly listen and attempt to understand.

One way to increase the likelihood that the listener will indeed listen is to give that person something to do when the speaker is done talking. For example, Costa encourages teachers to instruct the listener in a pair to paraphrase what the speaker has said by using the stem, "You're suggesting . . ." or "You're proposing. . . ." (p. 135). The listener can respond to the speaker by asking for a point of clarification: "You mentioned _____. Can you tell me a bit more about that?" Both paraphrasing and probing in order to clarify allow the listener to truly seek understanding. Teachers who want students to paraphrase and otherwise seek clarification should take the time to model exactly what it is they want students to do. No assumptions should be made that students at any grade level understand how they should either paraphrase or otherwise seek to understand.

It is important to us as human beings that others understand what we communicate. Teachers should always take the time to discuss with students why this is so. Students who buy into the importance of clarity in communication are more likely to participate willingly and with an eye toward improving their own speaking and listening skills. Wagner (2008) points out that communication skills (oral and written) are critical to success beyond just college and the workplace: "The ability to express one's views clearly in a democracy and to communicate effectively across cultures is an important citizenship skill as well" (p. 34). It is, therefore, not enough that we work with students on these communication skills; it is important to engage them in a wide-ranging discussion as to why these skills are critical to *their futures* in society and the workforce.

Build Basic Social Skills

Classrooms at any level in the educational system operate better when positive, basic social skills are the norm. For example, in observing hundreds of classrooms over the years, I have noticed that teachers who greet students at the door and take the time to involve themselves in short, positive conversations with one or two students prior to the start of class set a positive tone for the rest of the class period. On the other hand, I have seen teachers who sit at their desks as students enter, grading papers or otherwise ignoring students, and I can predict with a fair amount of certainty that the social skills demonstrated by the students will be as lacking as those of the teacher. Once again, when we don't model what we teach, we are teaching something else entirely.

Teachers can help students practice basic social skills from the first day of school, according to Burke (2008), by having students spend five minutes sharing in trios something that speaks to themselves (favorite music, books, food). Teachers can model this, while demonstrating six social skills that will enhance the mini-presentations:

1. Introducing themselves appropriately

2. Maintaining eye contact with other classmates

3. Using positive facial expressions and body language

4. Answering any questions posed by their peers

5. Practicing good manners and being polite

6. Using first names when they interact with their classmates (p. 105)

Again, teachers should model this, first as the speaker, and then (with a student doing the talking) as if they were one of the listeners in the trios. While this is going on, teachers should walk around the room, listening to the conversations without being obtrusive. Listening carefully to the groups may raise issues that provide the teacher with ways to improve later on.

Remember, the key here is to improve the social skills of the students, no matter what grade level. They practice speaking and listening, while teachers work to help them improve. This should happen during the first week of school, perhaps on the first day. The reason for this is that teachers will, later on, want the conversations to be content oriented, and it is critical that the processes be established in such a way that students can successfully concentrate on *content* because they have the *process* down. The only way to get to this point is to practice, practice, practice . . . and give students feedback, feedback, and more feedback along the way.

Reaping and Sowing

One way to create a classroom environment conducive to progress is to make it possible for students to meet in pairs and groups without letting sarcasm and rudeness derail the discussions necessary to processing information. Student-to-student cooperation and communication require that they can take risks in the interest of learning without fear of intimidation on the part of other students in the class. I have seen attempts by teachers to get their students to share in pairs or groups fail for the simple reason that it was clearly not safe for them to do so in a basically negative classroom environment.

Teachers can disrupt the flow of learning in a classroom very quickly, through their own negative actions. On occasion, I have observed teachers who berate and belittle their students, thus breaking the rules of student behavior prominently affixed to the wall of the classroom. Burke (2008) affirms that reprimanding students in public has a destructive effect on the classroom environment: "Students do not feel free to engage in interactive discussion, contribute ideas, or share experiences if they are never sure when they will incur the teacher's wrath or become the object of the teacher's sarcasm or anger" (p. 85). Burke adds that showing respect for students "is essential for classroom management" (p. 85). Showing any kind of disrespect for students will derail any continuous-improvement efforts on the part of students. Further, disrespect aimed at students will undoubtedly be returned in kind; I have witnessed this again and again over the years. No teacher committed to the continuous-improvement process can allow disrespect and purposefully hurtful acts on the part of anyone in that classroom.

Show 'Em Your Cards

I am a firm believer in laying the cards on the table for students to see. Let them know why you—and they—are working together for their benefit. My suggestion is, rather than explaining everything to them, let them weigh in on why they think something they are doing is important. Why, for example, do you make certain that they move every few minutes? They will no doubt tell you—and it is true—that kids get bored sitting for too long. I have asked this enough of students to know that they respond this way almost every time. It is also true that movement releases neurotransmitters (dopamine, serotonin) that make cognition possible, and you can explain that to them. Either way, I guarantee that students of any age enjoy getting up and moving. I also guarantee that when kids don't move in a purposeful way that is engineered by the teacher, they will look for ways to move on their own—that pencil sharpener on the other side of the room is going to look mighty inviting.

Teachers might also ask students why keeping a run chart showing their own, individual progress over time might be a motivator. Teachers can discuss with students the value of collaboration, summarizing what another student says, asking a partner for a point of clarification, or the importance of showing respect for peers. I know teachers who involve students in the setting of class norms at the beginning of the year, and others who lead conversations on why students should be doing more work than the teacher. There are any number of value-laden conversations that teachers can facilitate concerning brain-based learning principles and intrinsic vs. extrinsic rewards.

Also, it is helpful if teachers avoid giving their own opinions about something before soliciting opinions from students. The problem here, as Brooks and Brooks (1999) point out, is that "students assume that teachers know more than they do. Consequently, most students stop thinking about a concept or theory once they hear 'the correct answer' from the teacher" (p. 107). If you ask students to stand, get into a trio, and then share what they know about a specific topic or concept, chances are that not only do many of them know something about it, but they can also share what they know with peers. There is a natural tendency for teachers to simply share what they know or understand first, and they will need to suppress that urge in order to discover what the kids already know.

When students are explaining, they are learning. When they are explaining, teachers are listening. Teachers must develop a capacity to listen without betraying any emotion by way of body language. One of the most effective educators I have ever seen has mastered the art of putting his hands at his sides, looking at someone who is speaking—all while betraying no judgment or any other emotion. He also does not say, "That is a great question!" to those who ask them. If teachers say that, they are judging, and if the next student does not hear that exclamation (and they do notice!), she is likely to feel that her question is somehow inferior. Being inconsistent with this kind of praise will not help engender the kind of safe classroom environment that accelerates the continuous-improvement process.

Asking Them Honors Them

On the last day of the school year, I handed my middle school students a two-page questionnaire intended to give me feedback as to how I had done during the past nine months. The questionnaire asked about many things related to my instructional delivery systems, my use of visuals, and tons of other things related to *how* I did *what* I did for them during the course of the school year. It was great for me, but it was utterly useless for them. I could use it to improve the following school year, but those who completed the questionnaire would be gone. They must have wondered, as I reflect on it now, why I had not requested their feedback sooner. Had I done this at the end of each nine-week grading period—at the very least—I could have made changes that would have benefitted them immediately.

On the other hand, I know a middle school teacher who has her students contribute a sticky note to a Plus-Delta Chart every few days during the course of the school year (Figure 4.1). On the left of this chart (attached to the wall of her classroom), each student places a sticky note that lets her know what, in their opinion, she is doing that they find instructionally helpful and efficient. On the right, under the delta symbol, each student has the opportunity to affix a sticky note that lets her know where, in their opinion, she might improve. I can say with complete certainty that *kids love to be asked what is working and what can be improved in their own interest.* Asking them honors them, and teachers can do no better than request their students' feedback as part of the continuous-improvement process.

One piece of feedback she received over and over again had to do with the fact that her students loved it when they got to do something that was truly hands-on in nature. They also enjoyed being involved in the decision-making process on occasion, as in helping construct a set of classroom norms at the beginning of the school year. It is with these stickies that she learned to increase the visual and kinesthetic while decreasing the auditory in her sixth-grade classroom. This teacher also learned that by letting them write on the sticky side of the note, their feedback was hidden from any set of eyes other than hers. Most importantly, her students enjoyed being able to assist their teacher in the minor or major instructional adjustments that would

Figure 4.1 Plus-Delta Chart

Student-to-Teacher Feedback	
+	Δ

ultimately benefit them. She learned that asking them honored them.

Final Thoughts

Teachers ought to spend a good deal of time in the summer thinking about what kind of classroom environment will speed students along the continuous-improvement highway. Teachers can remove barriers for kids, but they can also erect barriers that students will have difficulty surmounting or sidestepping. The teacher who yells at his students several times in September will single-handedly destroy all the bridges on the highway, and I have watched teachers do just that—and in the first thirty seconds of a class period.

On the other hand, I have seen cool, relaxed teachers at every grade level create the kind of classroom environment I would want my children to experience. These are classrooms where the students are engaged, not just busy, and visibly loving every minute of it. A fifth-grade student once told another administrator and me that she could not wait to get to the school bus every morning. In that same class, a student explained that he and his classmates were like a family. They looked out for each other, he said, and they all agreed, giving us example after example of how this was so. End-of-year tests were taken in stride in this classroom, and the kids hated to leave at the end of the year—and the parents hated to have them leave as well.

Teachers—individually or in tandem with colleagues—must think about what kind of classroom environment will facilitate the kind of social, academic, and intellectual growth that parents have a right to expect for their kids.

In Chapter 5, we'll discover the importance of managing process in schools as a way of creating a system of continuous improvement for everyone involved.

5

Systematizing Process Improvement in the Classroom

I can't count the number of times I have said or have heard others say, "Well, *there's* a process in need of improvement!" Whether it relates to transportation, the cafeteria, the physical plant of the building, communication, scheduling, assessment, or anything else concerning schools or classrooms, processes can always be worked on and they can always be improved. Conzemius and O'Neill (2002) affirm that "the key to making improvements is to begin thinking about your school as a dynamic organism comprised of many interrelated processes" (p. 191). Generally speaking, if these interrelated processes work well, then the school itself works well.

Process becomes systemic when reflection becomes institutionalized. When leadership in the form of teams dedicated to continuous improvement are constantly looking at results—and making necessary changes and adjustments—the whole process becomes systemic in nature. In this way, processes are put under the reflective microscope, results are measured, multiple data points are examined, interventions are introduced, and the improvement cycle begins all over again with more reflection. As we have said many times in this book, the continuous-improvement journey has no finish line; it is by nature never-ending, and the pursuit of quality is relentless. The idea is to take a systemic approach to process improvement, so that reflection becomes routine and *the capacity to make things better is built into the organization.* In such a system, individual leaders, supervisors, and teachers may come and go, but the organization moves ever forward.

If an energetic and magnetic school leader makes tons of changes during his three years as principal in a top-down approach, the likelihood is that those changes may not outlive his departure. If what gets done depends on *his* energy and *his* ability to convince staff that such changes are necessary, this is more or less leadership by whim. Changes are made and processes are improved only so long as he is in charge. Forward progress along a number of fronts in the building are likely to slow and perhaps stop altogether when he is gone. Such haphazard organizational growth is not effective over time—and it is not systemic.

In truly systemic improvement efforts, everyone is involved at every level of the organization in a collaborative continuous-improvement journey. In a study that included in-depth interviews with twenty principals of high-performing schools, or schools that had showed significant improvement, Blase, Blase, and Phillips (2010) found that all twenty principals

> designed "inclusive" leadership teams consisting of themselves, assistant principals, and relevant others who were drawn from all areas of the school; members were collaborative, problem-oriented, and unrelentingly focused on instruction. Leadership teams met regularly, established communication protocols, and coordinated work with other teams when necessary. (p. 69)

The empowerment granted to those teams "increased members' ownership of decisions, and this, in turn, substantially increased proper implementation of decisions" (p. 70). This approach is truly bottom-up; in these schools things get better and problems get solved because the art of reflection is built into the system. Getting better is not a one-time event, and in systems-oriented schools, answers to problems don't come cascading down from above, along with the order to snap-to and "win one for the Gipper." Once again, those closest to the problems are closest to the solutions; those who are most impacted by processes already in place may be closest to the innovations and interventions that will ensure forward progress.

Everything Is Related to Instruction

Taking a systemic approach to solving problems and improving processes affects the classroom in one way or another, regardless of what the process is or where it operates in the building. If a teacher has spent a good deal of time building a relationship with a parent who then has two negative experiences in the front office, that teacher may have to work hard to repair damage for which she was not responsible. Lighting that is allowed to be subpar because of missing or defective bulbs can result in an inadequate amount of light in classrooms. Inefficient processes in cafeteria lines can lead to tardies as students finish lunch late. Restrooms that are allowed to remain out of order for extended periods of time can cause problems for those trying to use them and still get to class on time. Exterior doors that should be locked, but remain unlocked during the day, can result in issues related to safety. These examples are all problems that need to be addressed in the short run, but they are also processes that stand in need of a *frequent and regular system of monitoring.* Hoping someone will lock the exterior door is no substitute for a reliable process that guarantees that all the doors that need to be locked actually remain locked. Teams devoted to improving instruction can look at anything and everything that even tangentially affects learning on a daily basis. These teams ought to be in the business of identifying, analyzing, reflecting on, and monitoring processes that keep teachers and students moving forward.

Those Closest to Instruction

Ineffective processes can reduce efficiency or bring learning almost to a halt in the classroom. The teacher who does not pay attention to individual classroom-management processes is going to have a rough time of it, and learning will suffer because of the chaos that may result from an inefficient or nonexistent management system. In a classroom where students can talk, interrupt, leave, and sleep when they wish, this lack of consistent discipline is going to negatively affect learning. In classrooms where teachers simply lecture their way through the class period or block, students may play the game by behaving and even smiling, but they may well have gone to a better place in their minds. They may also choose to act out as a way of varying the passive routine favored by the teacher. When the processes that are in place (too much lecture, too many worksheets) are weak or ineffectual, they cry out for the kind of systemic improvement that teams of stakeholders can provide, given the chance.

There are schools where achievement scores are high, faculty and student absence rates are low, the building is immaculate, the hallways are quiet even during the change of classes, the cafeteria is free of both litter and fights, and visitors are greeted at the front door with a smile and a handshake; it is a good bet that the leadership team in those buildings attend at regular intervals to the processes that can either accelerate or impede forward progress. Regardless of how many academic degrees have been earned by faculty and administrators, and no matter how much teachers know about their respective subject areas, inattention to processes can serve as a barrier to continuous improvement in the building.

There are teachers who know their content inside and out but who may decide at some point in their careers that teaching is really not for them. For many of these teachers, success or failure has more to do with process than content. A high school history teacher, for example, who chooses to lecture most of the time in classrooms where students are passive observers—not active participants—may find his career cut short because he is exhausted at the end of each ninety-minute block, after being "on stage" for the entire time. Getting kids to sit still and concentrate in the face of an information flow that goes in one direction—teacher to teenagers—is not only exhausting, the teacher may find it is not at all successful for the students or for himself.

Teachers who are desirous of change and interested in serious systemic improvement will find it necessary to take a close look at process and ask a few questions: How do I deliver content? How do my students *react* to how I deliver content? Do I get my students involved in face-to-face discussions with each other in pairs or groups? Do I change gears in class every few minutes? What are the mechanisms in place to track student progress over time? Do students track their own progress (run charts, for example) over the course of the semester? Are the transitions from seatwork to feetwork (standing, paired conversations, or charting at stations throughout the room, for example) smooth and quick? Do I allow enough time after asking a question so that students can really think and formulate an answer? These are all process-related issues and need to be dealt with regardless of the course content.

Investing in Efficiency

I worry when I see teachers and administrators blaming other teachers and administrators for the latest problem du jour. That blame can also be transferred to parents, central office personnel, and the students themselves. As we saw in Chapter 3, playing the blame game gets nothing done and provides *no traction whatsoever* for improvement. After all, if I believe that something that is not working is actually someone else's fault, nothing I can do will make the slightest difference—so why try? Playing the blame game is counterproductive; it results in no forward progress.

Even in schools where the environment is generally negative, individual teachers can move forward along their own continuous-improvement highways but only if they make a conscious decision to quit assigning blame *and instead begin to look at the processes that either do or do not get things done in their own classrooms.* Processes are either efficient or they are not; for example, either the third graders in Mrs. Bendert's care walk quietly and in an orderly fashion from her classroom to the library, or they do not. If they do not behave appropriately in the hallway for Mrs. Bendert, but they do for the reading teacher, Mrs. Scott, *then there may be much that Mrs. Bendert can learn from Mrs. Scott as it relates to the latter's process for moving kids in the hallway.* These are the same kids, remember, but whatever process Mrs. Scott has established works better than that used by Mrs. Bendert.

Let's look at the two processes introduced on the first day of the school year, one by Mrs. Bendert, and the other by Mrs. Scott. Remember, they have the same kids. Mrs. Bendert has them most of the day, and Mrs. Scott has them once a day for reading.

1. Mrs. Bendert introduces her procedure for moving through the hallways from point to point on the first day of school. Before leading her new students to Mrs. Scott's room for reading on that first day, Mrs. Bendert tells her third graders to follow her down the hallway, in single file and with no talking whatsoever. She asks if they understand; they all nod their heads and move out the doorway and into the hall. On the way, Mrs. Bendert turns around to see a couple of the kids paired up and whispering, but it is not too bad, so they continue to Mrs. Scott's classroom door. Mrs. Bendert thanks the students for doing a good job of traveling through the hallway and leaves them with Mrs. Scott.

2. Near the end of the class period, but with plenty of time to do what she has in mind, Mrs. Scott has the third graders stand behind their chairs, push the chairs under the desks, and then

line up at the doorway to the accompaniment of a song. She explains that the *only* time she will play that song is when it is time for them to line up. She then has them sit down once more; when they are seated and facing her, she has them stand behind their chairs. When they are all standing, she has them push the chairs under the desks, and they move to line up to the accompaniment of that same line-up song. Standing in front of the line, she explains that they will follow her down the hallway in single file. She further explains that they will remain quiet in order that students in the classrooms they pass can work uninterrupted. She then proceeds down the hallway. Within a few seconds, someone in the line begins to whisper and moves alongside one of his friends. Without saying anything, Mrs. Scott turns around and holds her hand up, at which point they all stop. She points back toward the room, and they turn around and walk back to her classroom until they are lined up again inside the room. Once again, she explains the process, and they set off down the hallway. This time, they get to Mrs. Bendert's classroom in good order.

The results were different, and they are related to process. Actually, the basic procedure for walking down the hallway is exactly the same for both teachers. The difference is in the execution. Mrs. Bendert *explained* the process to her students but accepted variations outside the norm as they all moved down the hallway. She figured that it wasn't too bad, really, and it worked out all right. Mrs. Scott explained the line-up procedure to her students, *but then practiced it until they had it right*. She actually allowed more time at the end of the class period to practice the line-up procedure at least twice. She would do the same thing during their second visit to her classroom, until they did it right and then *consistently* right. She did the same with the movement in the hallway. When they moved outside the norm, she simply had them do it over. She did not yell, nor did she scold. She just had them repeat it until it was as it should be—*and as it should be every time.*

The problem for Mrs. Bendert will come down the road a bit, perhaps several weeks into the school year. It did not escape the notice of her third graders that there was a disconnect between her instructions and the execution. They analyzed and then they inferred. They came to the conclusion that they could push the envelope. As for Mrs. Bendert, the few problems in the hallway were "no big deal" in her opinion, and she even thanked them when they got to Mrs. Scott's door. The problem here is that she thanked them for *not doing* what she asked them to do. She thanked them for *not* following the procedure. The gap between how moving down the hallway *should* work and how it *actually* worked will widen as the year progresses, and it will result in frustration for Mrs. Bendert in a way that it does not for Mrs. Scott.

Consistency in Support of Improvement

Mrs. Scott—and remember, these are the same exact kids that were with Mrs. Bendert in the morning—took a little extra time on that first day for process, because she understands that consistency is her friend. Processes must be monitored and evaluated on a regular basis, and Mrs. Scott was prepared to do that. Her students got the point; there was one way to do line up and move down the hallway, and when they stepped outside the norm, Mrs. Scott calmly had them do it all over again until it was right. Jones (2007) points out, "Consistency permits only two conditions:

1. You are consistent.

2. You are inconsistent." (p. 187)

Mrs. Scott was determined that her students understand the procedures related to the end of the class period and that they perform up to the standard. In the face of a *small disruption* in the hallway, she returned them to her classroom and once more explained the procedure. On the second try, they got it right. Mrs. Bendert was determined to get her students to reading class and ignored the small disruptions—the beginnings of inconsistency.

Small disruptions may seem insignificant in August or September, but Jones (2007) reminds us that "while a crisis can sometimes erupt out of the blue, most big problems are just small problems that have been allowed to fester" (p. 187). It is quite likely that Mrs. Bendert is headed for larger disruptions in the hallway (and in her classroom) in October and November, or even sooner, because the students inferred after that first iteration of the procedure that their teacher was being inconsistent in a way that would allow them to break the rules. Four or five weeks down the road, it is not hard to imagine that Mrs. Bendert might sit with her friends in the faculty lounge and complain about the way her kids walk down the hallway. Mrs. Scott proved that it was not the kids but *her consistently applied process adjustments* that made the difference. Again, the process was the same in each case: The students were to walk in single file and silently down the hallway, behind the teacher. It was in the area of *managing* process that Mrs. Scott excelled.

In this and other processes, teachers must be willing to take the extra time not only to *explain* the procedures to the students, but also to practice them until everyone is operating inside the norm. The trouble lies, as we have seen here, in the gap between theory and execution, between consistencies and inconsistencies when it comes to managing processes in the classroom. Wong and Wong (2005) affirm that "most behavior problems in the classroom are caused by the teacher's failure to teach students how to follow procedures" (p. 174). Explaining the procedures is not enough; it is in the rehearsal that students grow to understand how to do whatever it is that needs doing. Procedures that become habits and routines contribute to the smooth-functioning classroom (p. 174).

If Mrs. Bendert has problems with her students in the hallway down the road, it will not be because she is a bad person, nor will it be because her students are simply unruly. If the gap between the standard for moving down the hallway and the students' outside-the-norm behavior grows over time, it will be traced directly to Mrs. Bendert's inconsistent follow through. It is a matter of being willing to invest time during the first days and weeks of school to make necessary processes effective over the long haul. Mrs. Bendert cut corners; *Mrs. Scott did not.* Mrs. Scott was consistent in her application and monitoring of the process; Mrs. Bendert was consistent only in her inconsistency.

Giving Directions: Another Process in Search of Clarity

Another barrier to progress comes with giving unclear directions to students. Students have to know what it is they are supposed to do; when possible, teachers should give directions in writing. If directions are given verbally, then care must be taken to give only one direction at a time. This is no small matter, and it is something to which teachers often give little thought. While I was observing in one classroom, a teacher seated her students at the beginning of the class period, followed by what can only be described as a series of seven or eight verbal directions, given in rapid-fire fashion. On that occasion, I was watching the students while the teacher issued her instructions. Once she was finished—two minutes tops—she told them to go ahead and start the exercise she had outlined, while she circulated around the room.

What followed was as predictable as it was avoidable. Very few of them knew exactly what to do, and she spent several minutes walking among the desks in her classroom, answering questions from bewildered kids. It took several more minutes for everyone to become involved in the activity. During her travels around the room, the teacher's facial expressions and body language betrayed her annoyance. To her, the directions had been clear and unambiguous; to them it was a case of too many directions given too quickly for them to properly process. She could have slowed down, and she could have delivered each of the several directions one at a time, allowing her students to process and complete each one in turn before moving on to the next. She also could have given them a simple, written set of directions. Instead, their efforts at improving their reading skills (the object of the lesson) were disrupted and delayed because of the teacher's confusing first few minutes of class.

The entire process involved with getting into an activity is composed of several steps, and those steps can be completed one at a time. For example, if desks need to be cleared, students can clear them right away. The teacher need only look around the room to know that in a few seconds, desks are empty of book bags, lunch bags, and anything else students may have brought with them to class. If books are going to be part of the activity, a teacher can have students get them and lay them open on the desk to a specific page. One glance will then tell the teacher if everyone is ready to go. If student journals are going to join the book on the desk, Step 2 can involve getting the journal open to where the students were last working. Again, one glance suffices to assure the teacher that materials are in the ready position. Pencils can be raised in the air, a clear indication that pencils are poised and ready; one teacher I know has several jars of sharpened pencils, and the students each take one on the way in and deposit them on the way out. This way, she knows everyone is going to have a #2 pencil, and they will be sharpened. So, desks are cleared, books and journals are opened, and #2 pencils are both sharpened and ready, all within a minute or so.

Another way to handle this is to have a specific piece of upbeat music playing, while on the screen a picture of a student desk *as it should be set up* appears in slide form. The desk has a picture of the language arts book, a student journal, and a pencil (Figure 5.1). The only time the teacher ever plays that song is for desk setup. As a teacher greets students at the door, the music does her job for her, directing her students' attention to the screen and to the business at hand. When she walks into the room, the teacher—using her remote—swells the volume of the music, and then cuts it off abruptly. Looking around the room, she sees that almost everyone has the reading book, journal, and pencil ready to go on an otherwise empty desk. There was never any confusion, because the screen graphic communicated exactly what needed to be done. In a middle or high school classroom, when the late bell rings, everything is ready to go in terms of materials. The teacher can *then* have students turn to a particular page and section of the student journal and get started on the activity.

Figure 5.1

Photo by Kathy Galford

My suggestion would be that during the first week of school, whatever procedural norms are going to hold for the entire year be practiced several times until, for the students, they become routine. A sixth-grade teacher, for example, might take several different digital pictures of the way desks will be set up at various times throughout the year. On the first day of school, students can practice some of these setups several times while the teacher holds a stopwatch and encourages them to decrease the time needed to get everything ready on each occasion, all to the accompaniment of a song that will be used only for this purpose. Eventually, students will learn to respond to the song by glancing at the screen to see how their desks should look and act accordingly *without any verbal cue from the teacher.* Once this process has been made routine, it will save teachers and students a great deal of time during the course of the week, month, and semester.

Figure 5.2

Photo by Kathy Galford

Notice in Figure 5.2 how one sixth-grade language arts teacher has located

Figure 5.3

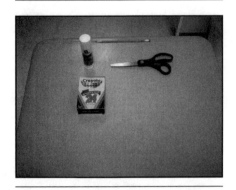

Photo by Kathy Galford

the materials most used by her students in a plastic bag to the right of each student's desk. Books used most frequently are on the tray under the desk, and on entering the room, students can look at the screen in the front of the room to see what is needed for the first activity (as in Figure 5.3, for example). The teacher meets students at her classroom doorway, and she does not have to tell them anything once she closes the door. The picture on the screen, accompanied by the setup song, told them everything. The bell rings, she moves into the room, and her students are ready to go. The only thing lacking at this point are the directions for the activity, directions she will give one at a time as she always does, in order to avoid any confusion. Her sixth graders love this structure, along with the clarity it provides. It is efficient and it is a product of much reflection and experimentation in the interest of continuous improvement.

Music to Their Eyes

In the preceding example, the use of an upbeat song caused students to glance at the screen. The directions (visual) for setup were clear and unambiguous. The musical cue told them where to look, and what they saw told them what to do, freeing the teacher to do whatever else needs to be done. This solves the problem, by the way, for teachers who want to—and they *should* want to—greet students at the door while those who have entered the room follow the routine with a little help from some great, upbeat music and a solid, clear visual.

One teacher I know uses a particular song to let her students know it's time to clean up, and a different song to get them lined up and ready to go somewhere else in the building. The power of the musical cue was demonstrated to her one day when she, unknowingly, played the wrong song. Glancing at the door to see that they were already lined up, she noticed that the tables in her room had not been totally cleaned off—she had unknowingly played the line-up song first, before the clean-up music. Her students responded as they had been trained to do, and it was an (unintended) lesson as to the power of routine.

The two songs she used, by the way, are lively pieces of music, and I have been present in scores of classrooms where students literally respond by grooving to wherever it is they need to go, or even singing along as they set up or clean up their desks or tables. In many cases, cleaning up the room is a function of the distribution of many separate jobs among the students. In one class, for example, when the music started, one student did nothing but pick up the pencils that students had taken out of the jar at the beginning of class. Two students grabbed paper towels and began to clean desktops, while others straightened furniture or returned to bookcases along the wall books that students had used throughout the class period. Everyone had a task, and the music cued the action.

Jensen (2005), in a book that suggests songs for every classroom occasion or mood, reminds us that music has the power to get us, collectively, "into the same emotional state, mental rhythm, and frame of mind. Music creates a harmonic beacon for our bodies to follow" (p. 1). Music is particularly effective as an accompaniment to movement within the classroom. Here are some places where *transitional processes* can be enhanced by upbeat music:

- Setting up for the opening activity upon entering the classroom
- Moving from chairs to standing pairs during a lesson
- Moving from standing pairs to quartets
- Moving from standing pairs/trios/quartets back to chairs
- Moving to and from the rug in an elementary classroom
- Moving to and from work stations/activity centers in any classroom
- Transitioning from one activity to another during the class period or day
- Getting into or coming out of a short break
- Moving from chart to chart in a walkabout activity
- Picking up the materials for an activity
- Cleaning up desks or tables before leaving the classroom
- Standing and moving to several points in the room to pick up handouts
- Lining up at the end of the class period or day

Each of these transitions is an individual process that must be explained and then practiced until it becomes routine. If those transition processes are not internalized on the part of students, the result can be chaos, *and valuable time will be wasted.* When that happens, teachers increase their stress level in direct proportion to the level of confusion displayed by students who may not be clear as to what is expected. Even the simplest process-related expectations must be absolutely clear to students at any grade level. This is critical, because collaboration in the classroom is important to learning, but attempts to get students in productive pairs, trios, and quartets for any reason whatsoever will flounder if attention is not paid to the processes that allow students to focus on content in those pairs or small groups.

Finally, like all processes, the use of music for transitions must be monitored and evaluated every time it is used. It is possible that each time the line-up music is played, the students take *more* time to get lined up along the wall. It may be that some students are ignoring the process and begin moving toward the door only when everyone else is headed into the hallway. If teachers allow this to happen, if they let the process become unraveled and undone, *there is no systemic approach to improvement in place.* In this case, as in the example of students in the hallway, what does not get monitored and evaluated *does not get done.*

Improving Information Flow and Processing

Early in my teaching career, communication in my secondary classroom was pretty much one way, from me to my students. I talked, and they listened. I talked, and they took notes. Then, it was much to be hoped that they took those notes, along with what they retained from my spirited and wonderfully informational lectures, home in order to process the information they had garnered into some new understandings that would serve them well in their chapter and unit exams. If they listened well and studied at home each evening, they would be able to give me the right answers I sought on those exams and quizzes.

It never occurred to me that my students could look right at me, pencil in hand, smile, and be in a better place in their minds. I never considered that trying to listen, take notes, and process information all at the same time can be frustrating at best; this even though as a student I experienced those same frustrations in class after class in high school and college. If I thought about it at all, I probably reminded myself that I had lived through it, after all, and that was simply the way it was in classrooms. It was the status quo, and who was I to argue with the status quo? This one-direction flow of information was *all I knew*; judging from what I saw, heard, and experienced in those days, it was all most teachers knew. Forty years later, a multidirectional flow of information within our classrooms still eludes us in far too many instances. The status quo travels well, and its roots run deep. Breaking the grip of the status quo is not easy, and it requires a firm and relentless commitment to continuous improvement—for teachers and students.

Information in a classroom should flow in all directions, from teacher to student and from student to student, and within trios and quartets composed of students. Regardless of the subject matter, students are asked to read a great deal. It is fervently hoped, as I did in my own classrooms, that students will take whatever book it is home, dispense with all other distractions, and reflect on what they have read. It is hoped they will ask parents when they are confused and stick with it when it gets boring. The truth is that in this electronic, multitasking world, moments of personal reflection may be few and far between. Teachers must provide time in their classrooms for the reading, and for the reflection on the reading, individually or in groups.

Keene and Zimmerman (2007) recommend that teachers "go about creating classroom structures that permit children to discuss, ponder, argue, restate, reflect, persuade, and write about what they read" (p. 165). Reading a section of content-laden material is not enough; students have to work with the material, and they need to process the information in pairs and groups. Listening to lecture is not enough; students need to reflect on what they heard, preferably in structured conversations where listening is as important as talking. Viewing a short video clip is not enough; students must talk about what they saw and heard in the clip. Teachers, for their part, need to establish ground rules for these discussions, so they do not turn into shouting matches or result in students not talking to each other out of frustration with what someone said or did that was clearly inappropriate.

Teachers must model the kinds of discussions that will permit the processing of new information. Norms must be established; listening without judging, talking without being sarcastic, and collaborating without rancor. I have found that students already know what it takes to collaborate effectively, even if they cannot articulate it in a way that adults might. Teachers can brainstorm collaborative norms, model them in conversations with other adults (with students watching), and monitor them to make certain that the norms, once established, are being adhered to in those student-to-student conversations. Once again, this is no different from the processes involved in traveling down the hallway, giving effective directions, or facilitating transitions. Isolate the process. Monitor its implementation. Evaluate its effectiveness. Make necessary adjustments in order to make it better. Along the way, collaborating regularly with peers is an effective way of constructing meaning, building on the old foundations of knowledge in the process.

Constructing Meaning Through Collaboration

Life is not a multiple-choice test; it is far more complex than that. Issues must be confronted, and problems must be solved. When answers are found to questions that perplex, the answers are not always right, and they are sometimes messy. When as human beings we are cornered, we need to be unafraid to seek help from others. When we are confused, our peers can often help us see more clearly. When I was growing up in the 1950s and 1960s, we had dinner at a certain time almost every evening, and kids and adults would sit around the kitchen or dining-room table and talk, question, share information, and sort through issues and problems in a collaborative fashion. This happened even when we went to dinner at the homes of our friends; the evening meal was sacrosanct, and it was spent in the company of others. It lasted almost an hour, and I can recall that the conversation rarely lagged.

In today's world, the evening meal may be eaten on the run, and it often comes in a bag from a drive-through window. It may be consumed quickly while watching television, or the adults and kids may actually be in different rooms. Breakfast may be something again grabbed on the way out the door, accompanied by little more than a hurried goodbye as family members head off to school or work. This represents, I believe, a change in the social status quo of the Eisenhower era, and change is not always accompanied by improvement. We learned to collaborate during those meals, and at those breakfast, lunch, and dinner tables, in a way that may be absent today.

It is important that children and adolescents have the opportunity to talk in ways that help them process information and build new understandings. Students enter our classrooms with varying amounts of information on this issue or that topic, and discussing what they know with other students allows them to share what they know, even as they take in what other students in the group may know about that same subject. In doing so, they should be encouraged not to seek right answers, but to simply try and expand their knowledge and understanding about whatever it is they are discussing in student pairs, trios, or quartets.

In my early years in the classroom, I believed that in doing the talking as a teacher, I was teaching; I thought that when my students were listening, they were learning. Deborah Meier, as quoted in Darling-Hammond (1997), turns my assumption on its head. Meier says that "teaching is mostly listening, and learning is mostly telling" (p. 130). If this is true, then teachers need to do more listening, and students need to do more talking—gobs and gobs of (structured) talking. If students are in pairs or small groups as they talk, teachers need to move around the classroom in order to listen to what they are saying. Much is going on there, according to Darling-Hammond (1997): "Teachers learn from watching learners as they work; students learn by articulating what they know" (p. 130). This goes against the grain for many teachers who, after years of doing most of the talking and little of the listening, have come to believe that telling is teaching.

Getting the Collaborative Process Right

Any teacher who is willing to make the shift from the "teller-in-chief" in the classroom to the chief listener must first confront a troublesome truth: Just putting kids in pairs or small groups is no guarantee that they will work or play well together. Without an effective collaborative process in place, all this may break down in short order. Remember, common sense tells us that if we have a trio of classmates standing together in the room, we want them to treat each other with respect, ask questions of their partners when they don't understand, share without dominating, and work their way through disagreements without winding up screaming or becoming abusive. Any teacher who attempts to simply throw students together without sufficient preparation in terms of process management is in for the proverbial rude awakening.

However, this does not mean that teachers should not get students to collaborate; it means that much must be accomplished on the way to continuous improvement in the area of student discourse and collaboration. In what Darling-Hammond (2008) describes as an experimental study in problem solving for sixth graders, "groups outperformed individuals, and then when students were given a new analogous problem to solve, those who had first solved the problems in groups performed at a significantly higher level" (p. 27). One of the indicators of success when students collaborated as part of that study was that "students attend[ed] to each other and to their work in common, as indicated by eye gaze and body position" (p. 27). This is critical to success, and students may be totally unused to attending to each other in this way. They may find it difficult, in this age of multiple images flashing by at the rate of machine-gun fire, to concentrate on what is being said by others in the collaborative group.

Success in this case goes beyond eye contact and body language, however. As group members generate ideas and, by so doing, take the risk of putting something out there that may not be accepted or understood, they need to know that others in the group will listen and withhold judgment. Members of a successful collaborative group need demonstrate that they can listen with true understanding and empathy. Costa (2008) affirms that participants in these group interactions should be "able to see through the diverse perspectives of others. They gently attend to another person, demonstrating their understanding of and empathy for an idea or feeling by paraphrasing it accurately, building upon it, clarifying it, or giving an example of it" (p. 33). More than just doing some surface listening and being polite, Costa says "we want our students to learn to devote their mental energies to another person and invest themselves in their partner's ideas" (p. 33). This begs that age-old question: How do we get our students to do that?

Modeling What We Preach

It is during the first week or ten days of school that processes are explained, practiced, and turned into routines that will help students access content later on. It is not enough to tell students how they should walk down the hallway, clean up their desks or tables, and—in this case—work productively with one another in pairs or groups. Teachers need to model this during that opening couple of weeks. Working with elementary students for two days on the fine art of paraphrasing what a partner just said, the teachers in each classroom modeled with me exactly how this should happen. We modeled it twice and then circulated around the room as students tried their hands at paraphrasing with different partners. If we detected problems in the execution, we modeled it once more. We also elicited *from them* why it is important to try and understand what someone else has just told you. These were third, fourth, and fifth graders, and

I can report that they really did know why paraphrasing might help with understanding—they just had not had the opportunity to actually *do it* before then.

This strategy is called Paired Verbal Fluency (PVF), and the example we used in our modeling had to do with our favorite meals. The teacher with whom I was paired described her favorite meal as I listened. Then, when she was done, I summarized what she said. Then, I described my favorite meal, and she summarized. Having demonstrated the strategy twice, we then gave the students time to think about their favorite meals, paired them up, and had them flesh out their own favorite meals and then summarize in turn. If teachers can spend a good deal of time over the first week or two of school on this, then PVF is available later in the year when it is time to check for understanding as far as a particular content-related topic is concerned. Notice that we dealt with the totally familiar (a favorite meal) before moving to content-based information. Describing a favorite meal can be followed a day later by explaining why they like a particular television show, story, or pet. In this way, the process horse comes before the content cart.

Success Story

From a structured conversation between two partners that is basically about themselves, students (once the process becomes routine) should be able to move naturally to discussing content-laden material. I observed a fifth-grade math class in the fall of 2010, a math class run by a teacher who is constantly in continuous-improvement mode. Joy White spends the first five days of school turning processes into routines for her fifth graders. As part of that critical first week in September, White plays an upbeat song while her students move around the room and talk with each other. When she hits the pause button using her remote, White's students stop and face her, ready for her next command. She has them rehearse this process repeatedly during the first two days of school, until it becomes routine. White calls this process "freeze dance," and her students love it, and respond immediately when the music stops.

During the time I was in White's classroom, the content she wanted to review with them concerned multiplication; specifically, what is important to remember when multiplying whole numbers? What many teachers will do at this point is to ask the students (while they are seated), "Who can give me two important things to remember when multiplying whole numbers?" Before she understood the power of simultaneous, structured conversations between partners, White would have done just that: ask the question to the entire class, and hope someone can give her the answers she seeks. The problem with this is that it exempts almost everyone from thinking; the teacher is normally going to go for a student who (1) knows the answer and (2) has her hand in the air. There are always five or six kids in almost any classroom who *know* the correct answer, so most students can simply kick back and relax, safe in the knowledge that someone else will take care of it. Because she took the time to reflect on her lack of success with this largely passive method of questioning, and because she was willing to experiment with PVF, White found that it was far more powerful to have half her students talking and half listening, the latter knowing they would have to summarize (or add something to what the speaker in the pair forgot to mention about multiplying whole numbers). In PVF, the listener can't simply tune out; she has a task to perform when the speaker is done. The speaker speaks, and then the listener summarizes or adds to what her partner said.

When the paired conversations were done (three or four minutes total), White stopped the music, and her students finished their conversations quickly and turned to face her. Using another upbeat piece of music, she got them to their seats and then asked several students to share what they discussed. In the course of just a few minutes, every one of her twenty-plus students had the opportunity to weigh in with a partner on the question at hand, and every one of them had the opportunity to summarize (a form of paraphrasing) or add something to the paired conversations. Once they were seated (and it did not take them more than a few seconds to get back to their desks), she could debrief with them concerning content and process.

White has also developed, with the input of her students, a short list of powerful listening skills that she reviews with them before they work in pairs or groups. This important checklist serves her students well as they work on improving their listening skills as partners or members of a team; the list includes eye contact, body language, and appropriate facial expressions. White's next step in the process is to have her students use the list as an evaluative tool after they work collaboratively, so they can make necessary adjustments and improve those listening skills over time.

Joy White has put in place a set of processes that keep her classroom running smoothly and efficiently; her fifth graders are engaged and active learners in a system where their teacher facilitates process, while they do the work. White is constantly reflecting on process, tinkering around the edges or making wholesale changes, looking at the data, and evaluating the results on her continuous-improvement journey. Importantly, her students are an integral part of what is a collaborative effort.

Final Thoughts

I have been in classrooms where it is completely obvious that teachers have devoted a good deal of time to process management during the opening days of school. I know, in those cases, that every single process that is working well has been explained, rehearsed, and adjusted over time. In less-successful classes, my observation is that although teachers may have *explained* what students were to do early on, the modeling, rehearsing, and evaluating with necessary process improvements *did not follow*. I have heard frustrated teachers tell kids, "I told you how you were to do this!" When I hear that I am reminded that telling isn't teaching, and there is no substitute for strong, well-learned processes in the classroom.

In Chapter 6, we'll explore the notion that although there is no real finish line in the continuous-improvement journey, there are signposts along the way that can assist students and teachers alike in finding out just how far they have come.

6

Facilitating the Long Haul

I magine, if you will, that a high school cross-country runner has just come across the finish line in the district meet, and he has a *feeling* he has run his best race. He walks over to his coach and asks for his time.

"Well," says his coach, "you did really well!"

"Thanks coach, but what was my time?"

The coach responds, without hesitation, "I think this was your best effort yet. We didn't actually time it, but we can check with the course officials. Well done!"

History has not recorded the young cross-country runner's reaction, but disbelief and disappointment might be near the top of the list. Of course, no coach in charge of any runner on any track or cross-country team would go anywhere without a stopwatch; the coach wants that data point. If the runner who completed that race ran his best time, he wants to know how that compares to his last time and the times before that. Interestingly, he may have won or not won the race, but the fact that he broke his own personal best time for that distance provides a great deal of satisfaction. Added to other data points, that runner's time provides necessary feedback over time, and those data points taken together tell a story and give coaches and runners alike what they need to make adjustments and decisions.

Four of us, friends from high school and former runners on our high school track team, all meet each year at the Pennsylvania Interscholastic Athletic Association (PIAA) state track meet held annually at Shippensburg University on Friday and Saturday of the Memorial Day weekend. We sit in the same place in the stands, and we watch all the best runners, jumpers, throwers, and pole-vaulters compete over two days. My friends were distance runners in high school, and during the 1600-meter and 3200-meter races, they always measure the split times of the runners. On occasion, there may be a coach of one of the lead runners sitting next to us, someone who knows what that runner's split times usually are. Early in the race, armed with that information, that coach can sometimes predict what the time for that runner might be. For us as spectators, this provides an added dimension, and the data provided by that coach can combine with what we are observing firsthand to inform our own predictions.

Coaches, in fact, are obsessed with data. They hunger for all kinds of data, and every kind of evidence is worked into the calculus that informs their coaching decisions. They discuss the data with the runners, basketball players, and golfers with whom they work in order to inform their practice. Coaches want to know everything about their players, from their health to their eating and sleeping habits. They want everything measured, and they want the measurements compared over time. What shape is the field or track in? What is the weather going to be like, and how does Eddie perform in the rain or in cold weather? Our old high school coach from the 1960s is still coaching in his eighties, and it is a pleasure to hear him speak the language of improvement.

I don't care how young or old someone happens to be, it is wonderful to better one's performance in something; it is the measurement that informs, and it is the progress that inspires. The progress can be that of an individual or of a team, but knowing exactly how one has done, and knowing that the results are an individual or team best, provides deep satisfaction for the individual, the team . . . and for the coaches who hunkered down over every piece of data available, worked every angle, and maximized the strengths possessed by the athletes under their tutelage. With the best coaches—and with the best teachers, I believe—there is an almost messianic devotion to data and details. They celebrate success and then they move on because they know the journey never ends. They know that the biggest room in the world is the room for improvement.

One Foot in Front of the Other

Even the longest journey can be cut into segments, and there is a feeling of accomplishment when each of those benchmarks is reached. Students working on an essay want to know how they are doing along the road from the original set of directions to the final product. Teachers can use data to determine how well the class is doing in relation to where it began regarding its collective understanding of a particular topic or concept. A basketball coach uses statistics and observational evidence to determine what kind of adjustments need to be made, on an individual and team basis. Excellent administrators, teachers, supervisors, and coaches all use gobs of feedback in order to let those for whom they are responsible know how they are doing—and what needs to be done to move forward on an improvement continuum.

In the classroom, teachers can provide a great deal of feedback in the form of written comments that tell the student exactly what is incorrect, along with what could be done to correct it. Checklists can provide students with a list of things that need to be done in order to complete a task or class project; checklists can also demonstrate for day and night custodians exactly what needs to be done. Rubrics can give students direction on just what constitutes an excellent essay. In this chapter, we'll explore the nature of feedback in making consistent progress toward clear outcomes and high expectations.

We'll also look at the role of employee and student feedback in the pursuit of excellence. Graduates can provide school districts with valuable information that can assist in the continuous-improvement efforts at all levels. A big question for graduates is this: How well prepared for the world of work are they? Are there areas of strength and weakness that can inform improvement efforts on the part of school districts? Feedback from *current* employees takes the guess-work out of wondering what they think about how they are faring in the organization. Is it their perception that sufficient support is being provided, support that will contribute to their success along with the ultimate success of the organization? Seeking the opinions of employees also informs leaders as to how the organization itself is doing in the eyes of those most intimately connected to the processes and systems in place and functioning at any given time. At the classroom level, I have always found that students are eager to provide feedback that will help their teachers, although they are sometimes surprised that someone is asking for their opinions. Although we might not often acknowledge this salient fact, students *do know* what makes a good teacher; they also are under no particular illusion as to which members of the faculty are less than successful at reaching and teaching kids.

Employees and students alike want to know how they are doing. They would like to know how far they have come and where they are on their own continuous-improvement journeys. We all like to know that we are making progress, and we all like to know that we are *capable* of getting better at whatever we do, even though the rate of progress for someone naturally skilled at writing may be faster than for someone less able to put together a Level 4 essay. As a seventh-grade teacher on an inclusion team in the early 1990s, I can remember with a great deal of satisfaction the considerable progress made by a dyslexic student in his writing assignments over the course of a year. It took him much longer to construct those assignments, but he never flagged; he, his parents, and everyone on our seventh-grade team celebrated his progress. Lots of written feedback from me, some timely peer editing, his parents' support, and his own determination to do the job resulted in a very good paper. It wasn't a Level 4, but it showed great progress for someone who initially doubted he could make the progress he made over time. His initial successes accelerated his own continuous-improvement journey.

Accentuate the Areas of Strength

It is important to understand that each of us has areas of strength and weakness, and I, for one, never suffered under the illusion that I would be an accountant, a math teacher, or an engineer. I had a high school math teacher who pretty well understood this, and although she worked me hard, she acknowledged to me and to my Aunt (with whom I lived at the time) that I was probably not going to find fame with the world of numbers and formulas. On the other hand, several of my teachers encouraged me to develop what they recognized as a strength: language, both oral and written. My own continuous-improvement journey in the area of math was full of stops and starts; I did what I had to do and little more. My personal journey in the area of oral communication and writing proceeded at a much faster rate, and it was accelerated by teachers who understood where my capabilities lay.

It is the job of teachers at every level to identify the strengths of their students and then do what is necessary to accelerate growth, while working with those students to do as well as they can in areas of relative weakness. Along that highway, teachers need to erect signposts (checklists, rubrics, written feedback, run charts showing progress over time, formative assessment pieces) that benchmark progress in concrete terms. High school students who are given a term-paper assignment in September but receive only *reminders* along the way that it is due in December are more likely to set everything aside until the last few days—or forget about it altogether. Students who are not really clear about what is expected are less likely to want to complete the task.

For the best language arts teachers, the act of constructing the term paper is its own continuous-improvement journey. In this case, it has a clear outcome, and students have the benefit of plenty of checkpoints, along with a checklist and rubric, and plenty of interim assignments (collection and evaluation of sources, completion of various drafts) for which the teacher gives—as any good coach does—plenty of written and oral feedback. These teachers understand clearly that it is not about the term paper; it is about the development of the skills necessary to *create the term paper* and the internal rewards that come in bunches along the way—all this accelerated by a consistent and effective *process* for providing feedback. The discipline necessary to create an excellent term paper using a clear step-by-step process will serve students well in the world of work and in life in general.

Communication is key to the improvement process in areas other than the classroom as well; improvement teams hard at work on key processes need to be able to gauge how they are doing. If bits and pieces of the overall plan from that team are being implemented, they and everyone else need to know how it is going. This can be a critical and effective accelerant to improvement; if something that the team worked hard to come up with has been put in play, and if it is working, communicating and celebrating that fact encourages them to keep going. It also lets them know that plans are only effective if they are implemented, and implementation does not have to come all at once. Small successes lead to more success; if there were cynics on that particular team, they now have proof that problems *can* be solved and processes *can* be improved through collaborative action.

The key to continuous-improvement success in any part of the building—from the front office to the classrooms—is a commitment on the part of those guiding the process to set clear expectations and to provide benchmarks on the road to progress. Students and employees alike need to know how they are doing, how far they have come, and how far they have to go. Teachers and school leaders have an obligation to provide clear signposts along the continuous-improvement highway.

The Power of Wow

When I worked as a sales representative and sales manager for an educational-products company, the highlight of the year for me came at our annual convention in January. This was, of course, an opportunity to get together with people whom I saw only on this one yearly occasion. On the last morning of the convention, we all gathered in a large ballroom in order to see the collective sales figures for the year. We may have known roughly how well we had done as a company, but it was not until the room darkened and the screen lit up with a bar graph showing progress over time that we cheered and offered high fives all around. Sales increased for every year I was with the company, but it was in that one moment, with that one simple bar graph image, that it all came together. Visuals are powerful, and they were proof positive that we were headed in the right direction.

That same dynamic can be captured in the classroom. I have visited many classrooms where the teachers have a run chart on the wall, showing academic progress for the class as a whole. The dynamic at work there is *not* competition, but collaboration. One elementary teacher posts his students' collective progress in math and reading scores every month. He has the kids set a goal for the class; rather than *telling* them they have exceeded the goal, he *shows* them on a bar graph that he uncovers on the overhead projector. When he does this, there is pandemonium in the classroom while the kids celebrate. He relates that he just stands next to the overhead projector and smiles, letting the celebration continue for a minute or so. His kids feel like I did when I saw that bar graph showing sales success stretching over many years. The spontaneous high fives in both cases came because *we* did this—we, the kids in that teacher's classroom, or we, the sales representatives in that darkened ballroom.

In one high school science classroom, the teacher has a run chart on the wall that records progress over time for the entire class—not as individuals in *competition* with one another, but with an average grade to which everyone in the class contributes with his or her own individual effort. These kids are not scrambling over each other "on the way to being Number 1" in the class; they are working together to improve their collective effort over time. They help each other as a matter of design and a matter of course, as I observed, and when the dot on the run chart drops rather than rises, the teacher brings the entire class together for a discussion about what happened. They search for root causes; she does not accept excuses, and they don't offer any. They just work on how to bring that next dot on the chart back *up* again.

One of the great things I have observed through the years is that when students are involved in a collaborative effort toward a common goal, individual competition takes a back seat. In one middle school social studies classroom, the teacher made the mistake of posting *class* assessment results for all four classes on the wall in his classroom (*not* individual scores, but a score that represented a class average). You might guess what happened over time. The class with the consistently lowest average score began to think of themselves as "the dumb class." The teacher realized that the competition he had eradicated in each class was playing out to negative effect from one class to another. From then on, he took the average of all four classes and posted that run chart, making it a total collective effort for the entire team . . . with positive results. All four classes could now say, "*We* did that!"

In each case, from the sales convention to the elementary classroom, from the one high school science class to the four middle school social studies classes, *it was the visual bar graph or run chart that carried the impact*. I have seen teachers post a visual and then reduce the impact by talking about it before students have had a chance to take it all in and process its impact. Let the visual speak for itself. A run chart or bar graph that shows steady progress over time for any individual or group of individuals is powerful—I call it the "wow" factor. When revealing such charts, there are four objectives:

1. Let them see and digest it.

2. Let them celebrate progress.

3. If the collective scores went up, explore what caused the rise; if they went down, work with students on finding out why that happened.

4. Challenge them to do better next time, and let *them* set a realistic goal.

As to that fourth point, the only thing I have found more impactful than improving performance from one data point to the next is to exceed an agreed-upon goal in the process. Never underestimate the power of the group, and never underestimate the power of visuals in delivering a clear and positive message.

The "Cram Factor" as an Impediment to Improvement

I used to give vocabulary quizzes every week. I graded them, posted the scores, and assumed that those scores were an indicator of just how well my students were able to spell or understand those words. Silly me. Informing them on Monday of the quiz on Friday, I wanted my students to study a bit each night, committing everything to memory in small chunks. I *wanted* them to do that, I *instructed* them to do that, I *reminded* them to do that, and I *willed* them to do that!

But they didn't do that—at least for the most part. What many or perhaps most of my students did was to cram those words into short-term memory the night before, or the morning of, the quiz. They took the quiz on Friday, I graded them on Saturday and posted the grades on Sunday, and we all moved on to a new week and a new list of ten vocabulary words. The words and their meaning passed out of memory in a short period of time, for the most part, because my instructional-delivery system did not allow for any more lasting alternative.

In a powerful and instructive story told in Appendix D of this book, a Texas second-grade teacher, Jeff Carrus, introduces vocabulary words and, having posted the words on a chart, his students refer to those words and use them as they write and talk about what they have been reading. Their classroom reading provides rich context for the words. Carrus also has them draw pictures with balloon captions that provide a specific and powerful visual context for the words. (I have provided examples of that student artwork in Appendix D.) Carrus has his second graders *revisit* the words in many ways over the course of several days. Medina (2008) gives us some advice here, as it relates to memory and understanding, and it parallels what Carrus has his students do:

> Deliberately expose yourself to the information if you want to retrieve it later. Deliberately re-expose yourself to the information *more elaborately*, and in fixed, spaced intervals, if you want the retrieval to be of higher quality. Deliberately re-expose yourself to the information more elaborately, and in fixed,

spaced intervals, if you want the retrieval to be the most vivid it can be. (p. 133)

Because his goal is for his students to truly understand and be able to use the words, and not just regurgitate them on a quiz or test (as I did early in my teaching career), Carrus invests a good deal of time providing context for the words, and he constantly re-exposes them to each set of vocabulary words in spaced-out intervals over the course of many days. Those second graders experience success, and as we'll see in Appendix D, his students' parents love how he approaches vocabulary *and are amazed and delighted at the frequency with which their children use the words at home.* His students' understanding of what they read is enhanced and enriched because Carrus exposes them and re-exposes them to their vocabulary words over time.

Facilitating Quality Work

Teachers need to take care that they do not become the quality-control department for their students. Deming (2000) lamented that such departments in the world of manufacturing "have taken the job of quality away from the people that can contribute most to quality" (pp. 133–134), and that includes the employees on the production lines. If the production-line worker knows that the quality-control department is going to check everything at the end of the process, *there is no need for him to concern himself overmuch with quality at his position in the line.* The problem with this, of course, is that if quality is not taken care of at every point in the production process, the company may have to go to great expense to either remanufacture something or issue a tremendously expensive recall of the product, with all the attendant public-relations problems that entails.

There is some similarity between the lack of an ongoing quality-control system in the manufacturing process and the lack of an ongoing quality-control system in the production of student work. In the course of writing a term paper, for example, teachers are hopeful that Eddie will both improve his writing skills and develop an understanding of the content related to the topic. The most inefficient system related to the production of a term paper is the one where the directions are given by the teacher in September and the finished product is handed in to the teacher (quality-control expert) in December, with nothing more than reminders and verbal encouragement ("Remember, I expect each of you to do his or her best on this project! You have only six weeks left, so do whatever you need to do to get the paper to me on time"). If the student, like the production-line worker, knows there is someone at the end of the line who will check for quality, there is no need to do much checking along the way.

Student Checklists

The problem, of course, is that while the teacher has in her mind exactly what constitutes an excellent term paper, students may have only a vague notion of what a quality product actually looks like. Also, while the teacher's preproject directions may seem perfectly clear to the teacher, they may be less than clear to the students. Students must know exactly what is expected, and that can begin by providing them with some quality term papers that let them visualize the standard. If everyone in the class has read the same term paper, groups of students can work together to decide what *makes* it an excellent paper. What they come up with in their groups can be shared with the entire class, and those conclusions can be squared with a rubric later on. The important thing is to *let them grapple with the aspects of quality before all is revealed by way of a checklist or rubric.* If the directions are written, perhaps posted on the teacher's website for students and parents to see, the next step may be a checklist that allows students (and parents) to make certain everything is getting done—and getting checked—at every point along the production line.

As we saw in Chapter 5, so much is about process; in writing a term paper, we have the conjunction of process and content. What if we had a way to ask some questions of the student (and, once again, the parents if they choose to be involved), questions that would provide a scaffold for creating the kind of quality paper the students read before getting involved in the project? What if students could complete one step in the process and then check it off? What if the teacher could, by sampling in her four classes (of eighty-five total students), sit down with various students at intervals and accelerate progress with some simple quality checks? The good news is that checklists can provide this very structure.

Burke (2006) describes a student checklist as "a roadmap so students know the process for completing a complicated task" (p. 102). Checklists can, and should, be tied to whatever standards are in play, and that includes the writing of papers. Teachers can develop their own checklists from those standards and then provide a student-friendly—and very practical—checklist for use by students. In Figure 6.1, we see a prewriting checklist for a student research report.

Figure 6.1   Student Research Report Checklist—Prewriting

Standard: Students define and investigate self-selected or assigned issues, topics, and problems. They locate, select, and make use of relevant information from a variety of media, reference, and technological sources. Students use an appropriate form to communicate their findings.

Assignment: Research Report (prewriting)

Did you include the following?	Not Yet 0	Some Evidence 1
Select Topic:		
• Did you choose your topic from the list or obtain approval by the teacher?		
• Is the topic something that will interest your readers?		
• Is the topic something you are interested in?		
Ask Questions and Focus Research:		
• Did you list one or more questions that you want to learn about your topic? What are your questions? _____? _____?		
• Did you look at your questions to decide what the focus of your research will be? What is your focus? _____? _____?		
• Will your research report do one of the following? (1) address an issue, (2) solve a problem or answer a question, (3) tell about someone or something		
Find Resources:		
• Did you use a variety of resources to locate information about your topic? (1) newspaper, (2) magazines, (3) books, (4) Internet		
• Did you check the validity of your sources? 1. publication date _____ 2. point of view _____ 3. primary or secondary sources _____		

Did you include the following?	Not Yet 0	Some Evidence 1
Take Notes and Organize Information:		
• Did you take notes?		
• Did you organize and paraphrase your notes into an outline, chart, table, or graphic organizer?		
• Did you select quotations to use in your report?		
• Did you write down all of the information about your sources so that you can document them in your report?		

Created by Chris Jaeggi. Used with permission.

The teacher can make appointments with students to meet with them in order to go over the checklist and offer feedback and suggestions at that point in the process. Those meetings would provide students with what they need, which so often is an answer to the question, "How am I doing?" From the standpoint of the teacher who is sampling several checklists from her classes, she may be able to determine that several of those she has sampled are showing problems in the area of, say, checking the validity of sources. She spent some time going over this in September, but from her conversations with students, she sees the need to revisit this, provide some more examples, and allow for questions in order to clear up any confusion.

Again, in order for students to get better at writing term papers, they first have to know what a great term paper *actually looks like.* The directions must be clear (and written, perhaps on the teacher's website), and quality checks on the part of students (using the checklists) and teachers (going over the checklists with students) means that the finished products will be of a higher quality than if students are simply left to fend for themselves in the absence of processes that accelerate improvement. *Sampling* student work and checklists obviates the need for the teacher to check *every* student's checklist at every step, a seemingly impossible task for teachers who have little enough time as it is. My experience is that students who know the teacher is sampling every day are more likely to push themselves a bit more than they otherwise might. Quality is defined early and then checked frequently as a necessary and effective component of each student's continuous-improvement journey.

Checklists can be of value with any process in the building. They can provide custodians with exactly what needs to be completed in the week prior to the return of teachers, for example. Supervisors who take the time to develop checklists with employees have to spend a lot less time checking up on everyone. When everything on the checklist is completed, supervisors and employees can come together to talk about what worked well, what didn't, and what changes would result in a smoother process next time around. The introduction of this reflective and evaluative component—and then doing that consistently year after year—systematizes that process. The checklist can also serve as a formative evaluative tool for the custodial staff.

Checking Quality With Rubrics

The only thing missing from the preceding system is a rubric—in the case of the research paper, a writing rubric that, according to Burke (2006), is a "scoring guide designed to provide constructive feedback to students by helping them think more clearly about the characteristics of quality work" (p. 126). The rubric is divided into levels of quality, usually from 1 to 4 or 1 to 5. Students who are looking at the quality term paper provided by the teacher can have a writing rubric next to them as they work, and in their groups they can identify those elements that define quality in terms of style, structure, and grammar. With a *sample* research paper, a *clear* set of directions, a checklist, and a scoring rubric in hand, students are on the path to more self-directed learning and improvement. Add to those individual processes plenty of sampling and teacher feedback, and it all adds up to a powerful *system* that serves as an accelerant to the continuous-improvement journeys of students at any grade level.

A rubric can be applied to any process, including how a specific area of the building should look when teachers report. The checklist for custodians tells them what to do; a rubric would tell them how well they have done. A clean and shiny hallway floor, for example, provides evidence of Level 1 performance. A clean and shiny hallway floor without any wax buildup along the baseboard indicates Level 2 performance. A clean and shiny hallway floor, no wax buildup, and the completion of the job by close-of-business on a specific date constitutes Level 3 performance. With a clear rubric, quality is in the hands of those doing the work, whether we are talking about students, custodians, or teachers.

The best teacher-evaluation systems contain clearly defined rubrics, where teachers understand what constitutes Level 1 performance in the area of professional development or instruction. Districts that take the time to develop such evaluation systems are doing a great service to teachers and students. When I first started teaching, we received a single-sheet evaluation form with a yes or no circled for such things as *Communicates a professional demeanor* or *Builds rapport with students and peers.* Seeing that completed form in my mailbox told me that I was on solid ground with the administration, but it gave me no usable feedback at all. Schools that have developed rubrics—and then worked hard to make sure teachers understand what is in them—have really taken the on-ramp onto the continuous-improvement highway. Teachers have every reason to be optimistic when they know exactly what is expected of them in every important performance category.

If rubrics are developed for teachers as part of the overall evaluation system, administrators should accompany the rollout of the system with videotapes of classroom instruction that demonstrate for teachers what each level of the rubric looks like. Every building administrator responsible for evaluating teacher performance should also view those videos and attempt to place what she saw on the rubric dealing with classroom management, instructional delivery, or teacher–student rapport. Administrators and teachers need to understand the difference between a Level 2 and a Level 4 performance in each category before the system is formally activated. Wherever rubrics are used in the building, time must be spent making certain those for whom they are intended understand what they need to do to reach a particular level of performance. Students who spend time reading several essays and then work collaboratively with peers to determine where those papers fall on a four-point rubric are much more likely to be able to edit and adjust their own writing when it counts. Teachers who understand the difference between a Level 1 and a Level 3 when it comes to classroom management are in a much better position to self-evaluate and self-adjust in their own classrooms.

Goals, Feedback, and the Rise of Optimism

There is much to be said for optimism, and much to be learned from pessimism. Often, I have observed, school districts reveal master plans with lofty, overarching goals that may seem unreachable to administrators and teachers. It does not help that many teachers cannot make the connection between what is expected and what they have to do in order to meet those goals. That there are many pessimists and cynics when it comes to deciphering and comprehending a binder filled with objectives is not surprising. The big plan often never makes it into individual classrooms where teachers may have been operating in isolation for years. The district hands the baton to individual schools; building leadership introduces the plan, hands out the binders, and hopes that everyone will fall in line on the way to great things.

Would that this were true. I have yet to see a faculty march lockstep in any direction without confusion and the inevitable pessimism ("For crying out loud, not *another initiative!*") taking its toll, impeding and even derailing the entire program in the process. The job of leaders in any continuous-improvement journey involves dealing with teachers and teams of teachers at a microlevel, rather than trying to move everyone in the same direction at the same time, and the same pace. Conzemius and O'Neill (2006) contend, "Leading change is essentially managing one conversation at a time; reframing the conversation is a key skill and will require great empathy for how teachers are feeling (just as we feel empathy for our students) while insisting that teachers try again" (p. 155). In any given faculty, there are those who will embrace change with great optimism and much enthusiasm; others may be initially skeptical but require only the assurance of the leadership team that they will provide whatever resources are necessary in the way of materials and professional development. Still others have been down this "next big thing" road enough times that they may push back, initially and for some time, in the hopes that "this, too, will pass."

There is no one-size-fits-all approach to continuous improvement, and the goals of a brand new teacher and those of a veteran may be different. It is also true that every teacher on every staff in America has different talents and strengths. Gordon (2006) affirms that "For each of us, our most powerful talents represent the best developed neural pathways in our brains" (p. 94). Our relative speed along the continuous-improvement highway may well be determined by those strengths, and administrators who have become aware of those areas of strength in teachers can take advantage of that by helping them accelerate progress in areas of strength. The best principals I know are constantly in the hallways, in the classrooms, and meeting with teachers in order to facilitate improvement. When administrators get better, teachers get better; when teachers get better, students get better.

Over the years, I have seen teachers move from pessimism to optimism when, with the assistance of administrators or peers, they set—and meet—a short-term goal. The same is true of students. I once had a student whose mother wanted her to serve on my yearbook staff. Her daughter was generally pessimistic about her chances of success, and her sense of self-worth was low. Her writing skills were weak, but with help from her mother and me, her mechanical, stylistic, and grammatical skills improved. She received tons of written feedback from her peers on the staff, as well as from me. Eventually, she moved into a leadership position; during this whole process, her confidence level increased and her competence as a writer grew apace.

When teachers who are unsure of their capacity for change try something new, taking the time to evaluate it and making necessary adjustments along the way, they, too, build a sense of confidence and competence. The long-distance runner involved in the 3200-meter run breaks the race up into pieces and discusses with her coach her split times, when to lay back and when to surge ahead, and how to take the whole race one step and one lap at a time. She may set as a goal for the next race a faster first lap or a faster third lap. Progress in the front office, the lunchroom, or the classroom requires the kind of chunking that—when these small steps are successful—provides optimism and confidence for the next part of the journey.

Above all, teachers, teacher leaders, and administrators need to display an outward optimism consistently throughout the course of the school year. This should be accompanied by a relentless energy and enthusiasm that serve as a model for peers, support staff, students, and parents. I have been in schools where energy and optimism are palpable, and I have been in buildings where pessimism is king from the front office to the faculty lounge to the classrooms. Students need positive role models, and every adult in the building needs to understand that and commit to exuding energy, optimism, and a consistently positive attitude. Principals need not just to be seen in the hallways, cafeteria, and classrooms; they need to learn the names of the students, and they need to find out enough about those students that they can offer specific praise and encouragement as needed. Every adult should be committed to the relentless improvement of processes and systems within the organization, and visibly so. When benchmarks are met, when process-improvement teams are successful, and when goals are achieved, every leader's job is to acknowledge these critical steps forward in the continuous-improvement process. Unfailing optimism is part of the psychological makeup of every great principal, supervisor, and teacher I know.

Being consistently optimistic and encouraging does not mean overlooking poor performance on the part of teachers and staff. Improving processes and systems in the classroom and the building as a whole should remain nonnegotiable. Successful leaders, however, do not try to move the organization forward with threats, humiliation, or coercion. Such negative behavior is quite likely to increase isolation and inhibit growth by causing employees to draw inward and refuse to take the kinds of risks necessary for forward progress. The same is true in classrooms; teachers who exude pessimism and visibly negative behaviors are unlikely to experience much improvement in the attitudes or performance of students. Administrators, supervisors, and teachers who exude confidence and optimism are much more likely to inspire the kind of performance that moves the organization in a positive direction along the continuous-improvement continuum.

Working With Parents

Signposts along the continuous-improvement highway ought to be clear to students and parents alike. Teachers, from the preproject explanation to the submission of the completed work, can check in with parents by contacting a few each week. Using the term-paper assignment discussed already, a ten-minute conversation with a parent might include a discussion of the checklist that teacher and student went over that day in school. The teacher could request that the parent bring up the teacher's website as they speak, highlighting the checklist and providing some feedback for the parent as to that age-old question, "How is my son doing?" This kind of specific, substantive feedback for parents will help teachers build the kind of relationship that will support the student who is the focus of the discussion. Just as the cross-country coach saying, "You did well!" to the runner provided nothing that would provide traction for the runner's continuous-improvement efforts, telling a parent, "Eddie is doing really well on his term paper!" gives the parent some immediate relief, but nothing that can be used to further Eddie's forward progress.

Hargreaves, Earle, Moore, and Manning (2001) affirm that "reporting to parents is one of the most challenging and also most anxiety-provoking parts of teachers' work" (p. 188). Part of my own anxiety as a teacher came from the fact that I honestly gave my students very little useful feedback, and the grade or comments ("Good work!") on their summative tests and quizzes really did not give us—any of us, including parents and students—the basis for a substantive, meaningful dialogue concerning student progress. I would make statements like the following: "Eddie can do the work if he just puts his mind to it" or "Mary just needs to apply herself!" What would have been far more helpful is to contact selected parents and talk with them about the run chart that showed their child's progress in the area of writing quality essays, following that up with some discussion about the rubric-based formative assessments that is helping their child become a more self-directed learner.

Teacher websites can put checklists, rubrics, clear assignment instructions, and much else at the disposal of parents, no matter where their travels take them. Teachers need to think about making frequent phone calls to parents, perhaps one phone call during the day, along with one during the evening hours, that is part of a system of sampling. There is a tendency—and I contributed to that tendency until my last two years of teaching—to wait until there is a behavior problem in order to contact parents. At that point, the phone call is necessary, but it may also be nerve-wracking for parent and teacher alike, because there is no preexisting relationship that can make a trust-based dialogue possible. If a teacher has contacted a parent twice by December, and if both those conversations were achievement based and meaningful by way of feedback and helpful information, the behavior-related call in January will be much easier for the teacher and the parent.

I have found that a student who understands clearly that there exists a working relationship between the teacher and at least one parent is less likely to act out than one who knows there is no existing relationship between his home and the school. There is an opportunity cost here for teachers, of course. Many teachers have said to me that they would love to make those relationship-building, feedback-providing phone calls *if they only had time.* I can't say this emphatically enough: *Take the time to make the calls or visits.* Invite parents to school and discuss their students' continuous improvement in a way that answers the question, "How is my kid doing?" in a specific, meaningful, and actionable way. What they can do to help their children should be made clear, and the teacher's website should provide much valuable information that is easily and electronically accessible by students and parents.

Teacher–Student Conferences

One way to discover a student's strengths and weaknesses is through the use of individual conferences. An elementary teacher I know does what he calls *hunkering down* with his students. He will get down on one knee next to a student and use the opportunity to provide quiet, specific feedback, and to check for understanding. The other kids are at work on an assignment, and during those precious minutes, this teacher can see several students with an eye toward accelerating their continuous-improvement journeys with valuable one-on-one dialogue. He is not one to say, "Great job!" Rather, he will get specific in ways that provide usable feedback for his students. He does this consistently, and his students come to expect it—and rely on it.

Keene and Zimmermann (2007) point out that such conferences are "lifeblood to comprehension teaching" (p. 154). "Effective teachers use conferences to assess a child's use of what has been taught and to lead them to explore new applications and challenges," according to Keene and Zimmermann, and conferences end with "a discussion about exactly what the child will attempt next in her reading and writing" (p. 157). I can remember a high school English teacher who would bring us up front for some very specific conferences; with me, those short conferences often ended with a recommendation for a book or short story that I might enjoy. I took her advice on many an occasion; because she knew exactly what I liked to read, she would invariably hit the nail on the head. I still have a collection of Somerset Maugham short stories that came from one such conference. Teacher-student conferences can accelerate continuous improvement by providing students with specific information and feedback that allow them to make major course corrections or minor adjustments along the way.

Split Times and Final Thoughts

When my friends and I sit in the stands at Shippensburg University to watch high school students from all over Pennsylvania compete, I marvel at the amount of feedback provided for participants during the events. Runners competing in the 3200-meter run or 1600-meter run can see the split time of the leader when they complete each lap. Coaches stand along the fence and analyze how their runners are doing. Coaches for the pole-vaulters can now stand in a roped-off area on the field, so that they can give feedback to their vaulters after each attempt. The events are set up so that someone who is competing in a distance event and a distance relay gets time in between to recover—and get the kind of feedback from a coach that will impact his or her performance, later that day and in the future. The system is set up for the athletes, and their dedication and hard work is something to behold. They know what a great race looks like and they are coached by people who understand that anyone's best time, throw, or jump can be bettered over time. Great classroom teachers and building administrators provide that same kind of clear expectations, meaningful feedback, eternal optimism, and consistent support as part of the organization's continuous-improvement journey.

In Chapter 7, we'll look at ways individual teachers and small collaborative groups of employees can make a difference without waiting for a ribbon-cutting ceremony from the powers that be.

7

Not Waiting
for the "Go!"

Years ago, when I was conducting new-employee orientation
training for our school district, another trainer and I worked
with approximately thirty new employees in each orientation session.
These newcomers were classified employees from all over our school
district. There were secretaries, carpenters, plumbers, cafeteria workers, custodians, supervisors, and teacher assistants. One aspect of the
training was customer service, and it was always my favorite part of
the session. In these workshops, we distinguished between internal
and external customers, and we arranged participants in groups of
four or five at wall charts, where they discussed, charted, and later
reported on various aspects of serving each other, the students, and
the public (including "What is good customer service?" and "What
turns customers into raving fans?").

In those sessions, we invariably rediscovered what we already
knew: People can readily identify good customer service, and they
know when it is substandard. This is not rocket science; people enjoy
being treated with respect by those with whom they do business and
they resent being treated badly. Inside the organization for which
they work, people don't appreciate incivility from co-workers, and they
appreciate and respect leaders who have a zero-tolerance policy
toward that incivility. In our training sessions for new employees, we
collaboratively surfaced a set of core principles that could certainly

drive any organization, including the school district for which all of us worked.

These conversations were always interesting and invariably led to someone among the participants wishing out loud that his school or her principal or supervisor would do these things and adopt these commonsense suggestions in order to improve the overall climate and service of the work site or school building. My training partner and I would underline our belief that getting better in the area of customer service, positive behavior, and an improved work climate does not have to rely on orders from above or an invitation to improve how and what we do on a daily basis. Any secretaries who are the first points of contact for the school can take it upon themselves to make that first impression memorable and productive. I often told the (true) story of a building custodian who took time from his workday to have kids read to him on a hallway bench outside the main office. Another story involves a cafeteria employee who learned the kids' names and made them feel special every day.

It would be wonderful if every one of the thousands of school districts across the country would adopt as part of their continuous-improvement plan the purposeful development of a professional learning community (PLC), as outlined in any number of books on the subject today. It would be great if customer service was part of every school district's training program, accompanied by a commitment to improve such service over time. True *systemic* growth can only come from an improvement model that institutionalizes change on a large scale, but the lack of such a model should not diminish the desire of employees or small groups of employees to make progress in the areas of personal improvement or customer service.

Individual employees can seek to improve their own performance, increase their own positive impact, and help make the school a better place *on their own*. In doing this, they don't have to wait for the "Go!" Contributing to the overall success of the organization is possible without an edict from the front office or a mandate from the district superintendent. Working individually or in small groups, members of the organization can determine to get better at what they do and, by so doing, improve the organization. Progress need not be dependent upon *this* district-level program or *that* building-level initiative. I know teachers who, working with others at their grade level, have accomplished much in the way of continuous improvement. There are thousands of teachers around the country who have committed themselves to getting persistently and consistently better, as is the case with our fictitious middle school teacher, Julie, in the prologue and epilogue of this book. Julie knew that there was no overall effort to put her school in the fast lane of any continuous-improvement highway, but she refused to use that as an excuse not to improve her own processes and systems—something she was perfectly capable of doing on her own. She was driven by a desire to do better for her seventh-grade students.

Nothing is more powerful than an entire school dedicated to steady and sure progress for everyone in the building, including, of course, the students. Like Julie, individual teachers can improve *how* they do *what* they do without waiting for orders. Teachers who seek a path for improvement can find their own way, and it begins with a serious effort to look at where they are in terms of process, with a look at just *how well* they do what they do in the classroom. The key to success for those who make this commitment is to then put in place a set of processes that guarantees progress in the development of their own skills.

The happiest and most successful teachers I have met are those who are never really satisfied with where they are at any given moment. They are constantly trying to improve; they are constantly trying new things and are not afraid of change—indeed, they embrace change because they understand that progress is not possible without it. These successful teachers are also not concerned with making mistakes; they realize that mistakes are the lifeblood of improvement. Taking risks on behalf of kids is a sure path to betterment—theirs and yours. In the prologue, Julie made the decision, after three years of teaching, to do whatever was necessary to improve her own performance in her seventh-grade classroom. She knew very well that if she was going to become a better teacher, she was going to have to put the ball in play herself. Rather than making excuses, she made a commitment.

Like Julie, teachers and members of a school's support staff can do much to improve processes and systems if they refuse to wait for the "Go!" I know dozens of teachers at every level who simply said, "I can do what I do better, and I owe it to my students to reflect on *how* I do *what* I do." The principle that runs through every page of this book is that reflection, evaluation, and action equal improvement. Taking risks on behalf of children is what makes good classrooms great, and great classrooms even better. Don't wait, just go.

Looking for Like-Minded Change Agents

Over the years, I have found that when someone committed to self-improvement finds someone else in that progress-oriented frame of mind, great things can happen. Two teachers, for example, who are willing to open up about their own strengths and weaknesses can often bounce ideas back and forth to the benefit of both—and of their students—*even if they don't teach the same subject.* A fourth-grade teacher who has put in place a great system for teaching her students to write effectively has much to offer to a fifth-grade teacher struggling with relatively poor scores on the state writing test. The fifth-grade teacher, on the other hand, may have much to share when it comes to teaching math.

A group of three eighth-grade science teachers who make a commitment to meet once per week in the interest of continuous improvement may discover that there is synergy in multiple perspectives. It may be, for example, that one of the three teachers credits checklists and rubrics for her high science scores, and if she is willing to share this with her subject-area colleagues, they and their students can begin to benefit immediately. The key here is to get rid of this notion that teaching is a competitive sport; teachers willing to share what they have learned in a workshop or from a series of journal articles can serve as a change agent for any teachers willing to listen *and then act.*

These three middle school science teachers can go much further than simply sharing what works. The common use of standards-based checklists and rubrics by all three teachers—with an evaluation of their effectiveness in later meetings—can be followed by the development of standards-based formative or summative assessments to be administered in their classes. An examination of the test results, including an item analysis, can highlight areas of improvement for each of the three teachers in different areas. Common checklists and rubrics, along with common assessments, can serve to accelerate student improvement.

Common, formative assessments can be used by small groups of teachers to inform their own instruction and to gauge how students are doing relative to the state standards that drive the end-of-year tests. Teachers who deal with common standards can work together to develop these assessments early on in the school year; they can then administer them at the same time and compare the results. As Burke (2010) affirms,

When teachers receive the results of the common "practice" assessments, they use the data to adjust their instruction so that students both deepen their understanding of key concepts and are better prepared to take the large-scale and often high-stakes assessments. (p. 28)

If one of the teachers seems to have done better at teaching a particular concept, the others involved in administering these formative assessments can explore with that teacher reasons for his students' better performance. There may be other areas where he can learn from the instructional methodology of the other teachers involved in the process. None of this can happen, however, if teachers are not willing to examine and reflect on their own relative strengths and weaknesses.

A Willingness to Examine and Share

In all my workshops, I have teachers and administrators engage in group discussions (trios or quartets) about any number of topics. When they have finished with what was perhaps a two-minute discussion, I ask them all to raise their hands if they learned something new as a result of the conversation. In almost every case, at least two-thirds of the hands go up. Much can be accomplished if teams of teachers (department, grade level, vertical) take it upon themselves to meet regularly, reveal the processes they use, share perspectives, evaluate common data, observe each other in the classroom, and otherwise commit to collective improvement as it relates to learning.

In my capacity as a teacher coach, I often see two or more teachers approach exactly the same subject matter using different methodologies and with different results. One approach will engage students, while the other does not. Same material, different approach and results. I often suggest that several teachers at the same grade level each make a list of those strategies that work well for them. I then suggest that the teachers come together and compare notes. The next step is to take the time to observe the classrooms of those who are using a strategy that has been particularly successful. This means providing covers for a few minutes, but my experience is that teachers need to observe these lessons first-hand; it is one thing to listen to a colleague share what she is doing that is successful, but *seeing* that success up close and personal carries much more impact. It has the added benefit of bringing the teachers at that grade level closer together professionally, and even personally. Too often, teachers at the same grade level close the doors to their classrooms, and see each other only during faculty meetings or other schoolwide activities.

Teachers are sometimes reluctant to invest in the time it takes to collaborate with colleagues in the name of continuous improvement. Schmoker (1999) cites the example of an Arizona elementary school where the teachers overcame this reluctance, only to discover that "when they began to see collective progress, a direct result of their focused collaboration, the meetings became more meaningful" (p. 11). Schmoker goes on to say, "In the business of teaching and school improvement, intellectual capital—ideas, fresh solutions, and effective teaching methods—is the most precious commodity" (p. 12). I have observed teachers who are admittedly low on energy become truly energized when listening to those fresh ideas and solutions, along with successes in the area of teaching methodology, on the part of colleagues.

The Role of Leadership

I have said that individual teachers, or teachers working in small groups, can make a difference, even if their efforts are not part of a schoolwide, leadership-driven improvement initiative. I believe that supervisors in the cafeteria and head custodians can lead their own process-improvement efforts in spite of the fact that the impetus for such improvement has not come from school or district leadership. What is absolutely necessary is a realization that every process can be improved, from the amount of time kids spend in the cafeteria lines to the degree of cleanliness in the building's classrooms and hall-ways, followed by a commitment to take both action and risks on behalf of students. The fact that students deserve a graffiti-free rest-room should not be dependent on a districtwide initiative to rid rest-rooms of graffiti; I have been in middle and high schools where this commitment on the part of custodians to a quality environment is evident. Indeed, I once observed a high school restroom where fresh cut flowers were part of the décor, along with real mirrors and works of art on the walls.

That said, it is the role of leadership to lead in all these areas. By saying that teachers and other school employees can make a difference as individuals or in small, self-directed groups, I am not absolving building leaders from the responsibility of leading. Principals who demonstrate by their actions the value of collaborative learning and continuous improvement are modeling for teachers and everyone else in the building exactly how powerful such collegiality can be. Hord and Sommers (2008) remind us of the importance of developing professional communities devoted to learning, not just in words but also in actions:

> When the principal sustains focus on staff learning, student learning increases. Teachers who function at higher cognitive levels produce students who function at higher cognitive levels. If the conversations in schools continue to be organized around learning, this sends a message to everyone that the driving vision for what we do is learning. (p. 29)

A place to start for principals who want to walk the walk is with faculty meetings.

Many faculty meetings are not really faculty meetings at all; rather, they are administrative meetings intended to convey information. I can imagine a situation where principals call teachers together to decree that they will—henceforth and forever more—be a PLC. That done, the principal may begin telling teachers what they must do: collaborate effectively, quit teaching in isolation, improve instruction, and any number of other things that are part of a large "Thou shalt" list. The problem, of course, is that most of the faculty members have no idea how to break free of their isolationist chains—even if they wanted to, and that impedes forward progress. This whole first meeting, intended to kick off the PLC initiative, is anything but collaborative in nature, and it has the unhappy effect of providing teachers with a one-hour visual and verbal example of the disconnect between what is happening and what is expected to happen in the way of continuous improvement. Telling is not teaching, and telling is not training.

The key for principals is to commit to shifting the control of faculty meetings to teachers. It is difficult for principals steeped in the tradition of principals as the giver of information at these meetings to shift control to teachers. A former principal, Joanne Rooney (2006), shifted the focus at such gatherings from disseminating information to collaborative learning on the part of faculty members. Rooney thus moved from the front of the room to the side, and "faculty meetings became, in actuality, *faculty* meetings" (p. 91). In doing so, Rooney clearly demonstrated to her teachers that whatever progress was made would be made as part of a collaborative effort at professional development and continuous improvement. This may be a tough thing to do for principals, but it is an excellent way to send the message that forward progress is both collegial and nonnegotiable.

Meetings aside, the most effective building principals I know are also among the most positive people I have met. A principal who extols the benefits of collegiality and then trashes a staff member while standing at the soda machine with other staff members has just undercut—probably forever—any appeals to collaboration and collegiality he might subsequently make. The leader who treats an employee with disrespect, while sitting with that employee under a sign that says, "Respect is Job 1," is likely to get little or no traction with improvement efforts that require employees to follow her down the continuous-improvement highway. That particular highway is likely to turn out to be a cul-de-sac.

Keeping Isolationist Tendencies From Forming

I constantly encourage building principals to arrange—not suggest, but *arrange*—visits for new teachers in the classrooms of highly successful teachers. (Some would argue that new teachers should also visit the classrooms of not-so-successful teachers, so that new teachers can see what not to do. I disagree with this. If we have teachers who are known to be unsuccessful, we should take steps to make them more successful or weed them out of the profession, but we should not have new teachers spend valuable time in these classrooms. We need to let our new teachers see what our *best* teachers are doing.) Postobservation meetings should be arranged, so that the new teacher and the observed teacher can share insights as to what just happened in the classroom. These observations and the subsequent conversations between the two teachers can plant the seeds for other collaborative efforts.

Teacher mentors have a more direct role to play, and it begins with the nature of the professional relationship between themselves and their protégés. Too often, the flow of information is in one direction, from mentor to protégé. It is not enough to simply give advice to protégés and let them know the mentor's door is always open. This one-dimensional and decidedly shallow approach will likely not facilitate the professional growth of the new teacher. It is not enough to help her survive her introduction to teaching; the mentor's job, according to Lipton and Wellman (2001), involves an "understanding that the work is to increase their colleague's effectiveness as professional problem-solvers and decision-makers" (p. 1). Accomplishing this takes a commitment to a collaborative approach that allows for reflective dialogue, facilitated introspection, and not a little risk taking on the part of the new teacher.

Administrators and teacher mentors should commit to making certain that teachers new to the profession do not fall into the isolationist trap, where survival and finding out what is comfortable becomes the top priority. The teacher that is new to the profession is *not* a novice when it comes to being a student. There is a tendency on the part of new teachers to fall into patterns that are familiar from their days as students—lecture, videos, and keeping the kids busy day after day. Arranging for them to observe the very best teachers the school or district has to offer, involving them in reflective and meaningful dialogue about their profession, and making the mentor–protégé relationship substantive and learning focused are all ways of getting new teachers off to a great start. All these things are possible, even in the absence of an overall, schoolwide improvement model. Actually, this kind of attention paid to new teachers might well serve as a model for professional growth in the building as a whole.

This isolationist tendency applies not just to teachers but also to everyone else in the building left to his own devices in the absence of a dedicated model that actively and effectively works as an accelerant to professional growth and process improvement. No one in the building—students included—is immune from being held back by the drag imposed by complacency and the power of the status quo. Building custodians are perfectly capable of working in relative isolation for years, charting their own course and pushing back at efforts to disturb the status quo. Processes that could be improved in the front office may well go unchallenged and unseen, simply because they are never held up to the light and examined. Inefficiencies, even dangerous processes, in the bus loop outside a middle school may continue until something bad happens that gets everyone's attention and could have been prevented.

I have chronicled many examples of individuals who, by their actions and through a personal commitment to self-improvement or because they knew it would benefit students, have made a difference. I encourage school employees to continue to act and take risks on behalf of children and continuous improvement, even in the absence of a prime directive or a big school-improvement kickoff. It is heartening to know that there are teachers and other employees who, on their own and virtually without any outside direction or influence, will continually do things that support the district mission, vision, and core values.

However, as welcome as their efforts are, and as appreciated as they may be, their total effectiveness becomes a matter of scale. One elementary teacher can make a huge difference in the lives and intellectual growth of up to thirty students, year in and year out. One cafeteria worker can make a whole cafeteria full of kids love going through the lunch line every day. Three first-grade teachers who decide, on their own, to meet on a regular basis in order to improve their own performance can make a difference in the lives of all the students in all their classes. The music teacher who gives of her own time after school in an attempt to build a small, elementary orchestra can indeed become a positive force for improvement. Once again, this becomes a matter of scale, and we ought not to be satisfied to brag about all these people who, largely on their own, refused to wait for a major improvement initiative or the next best thing from central office.

Building administrators who recognize that it is the collective effort of the entire school community that will get the most bang for the buck must take action themselves. The main role of leaders is to develop leaders, employees who are empowered to take appropriate risks on behalf of the students they serve. Administrators must create communities where learning is what *everyone* does—not just the students. Isolation and the comfort provided by the status quo are impediments to improvement, and the manager-in-chief must become the learner-in-chief, modeling listening, reflecting, and collaborating on a daily basis. Individual acts can do much, but until the continuous-improvement highway is crowded with improvement practitioners, the status quo will be left largely undisturbed. It is beyond the means of individuals, no matter how well meaning and effective at a micro-level, to break isolation's hold on forward progress.

Breaking Isolation's Hold

Individuals or small teams, working independently, can do little to change the isolationist culture of a school. The school is better off with those dedicated and independent actions; the downside is that if and when those well-meaning people leave, the capacity for improvement they demonstrated goes with them. For a school to move forward in any substantive way, independent individuals or groups must be replaced by collaborative and interdependent teams that are all part of a larger system of improvement and professional growth, characterized by the collective pursuit of a set of common goals (Eaker, in Eaker et al., 2002).

In every part of the school, from the front office to the classrooms to the cafeteria, the focus should be on best practices. This means doing research that uncovers what works in each of these areas. Improving customer service at the building's entrance or office counter, for example, will involve researching the processes that are most effective for organizations, educationally related or otherwise. If the norms for customer service in this particular front office have evolved over time and in isolation, with no input or feedback from those who interact with front office personnel, then whatever system is in place may need to be held up to the light in order to examine, and possibly improve, that service. Any team chosen to examine front office service should be composed not only of those who work there but also of those who interact with front office personnel on a daily basis. Teachers, staff, parents, and students could all be part of that team; their perspectives are critical if it is they who are being served on entering the main office.

The identification of best practices when it comes to customer service may well provide processes that can be put in place a piece at a time, in order to determine their effectiveness. Changing the entire front office status quo in one fell swoop may be a case of too much, too soon. One small change—and one small success—at a time may build confidence and reassure front office personnel that well-thought-out changes can be both positive and effective.

Harness the Power of the Group

Individual teachers may want to improve but need the energy provided by colleagues in order to enter the on-ramp to the continuous-improvement highway. In an elementary school, this can be done by getting together regularly with grade-level colleagues in order to explore ways to improve the *how* of what they do. One group of second-grade teachers I know took it upon themselves to meet regularly in order to share ideas and examine the effectiveness of their own processes and instructional methodologies. Their collaborative efforts provided each of them with a source of newfound energy, and subsequent student successes resulted in even more needed energy.

Collaboration like this provides everyone involved with feedback and different perspectives they might not have had the benefit of while working in traditional isolation. Teachers who start talking with each other while focused on learning begin to discover all kinds of things they are not doing—but could do—and might even discover that some of their own instructional practices are, in fact, best practices. It may also be that much of the methodology teachers are using is inferior and ineffective, but they have no way of knowing that if they are working alone with the door closed. Schmoker (2006) states a sad truth when he says that what we have done is to create "a system in which generations of talented, hard-working teachers have engaged in inferior practices without receiving feedback that would alert them to this fact" (p. 24). Many teachers spend their entire careers without the benefit of seeing how other teachers handle the same content they are teaching. Administrators can provide feedback through formative observations, and feedback can come when one teacher observes another.

Our prologue's teacher, Julie—in a visit arranged by one of her assistant principals—observed the social studies classroom of a teacher in another school. Just seeing someone else handle the material and manage the processes she handled every day led Julie to question where she was in her own growth as a teaching professional. At the end of the third year of her career, she took the time to reflect on just how she might shift into continuous-improvement mode. While neither her school nor her district was embarked on any major reform initiative, the assistant principal's insistence that she observe one of the district's finest social studies teachers in action told her she would have his support and encouragement for her own improvement efforts. Reflecting on the data available to her from her own assessments and the state exams, she understood that something had to change.

Julie knew she was not a *bad* teacher; she just knew she could be a better teacher. In her conversations with the assistant principal who had made her observation possible, she grew to understand that continuous improvement means never having to say you're finished. It is ongoing and, in the words of Smylie (2010), "it is accomplished through small, incremental advancements" (p. 26). This is as true of teachers and support staff as it is of students. One way administrators can take the fear out of the next big thing is not to represent it as the next big thing. School employees who may be skeptical or even cynical about program kickoffs that resemble a Broadway opening may be perfectly willing to sit down and talk with an administrator about experimenting with some new ideas, strategies, and process improvements.

Julie's decision to begin to take stock of where she was and where she needed to go in her own continuous-improvement journey began with her conversations with the assistant principal; it was accelerated by her observation in the spring. Those conversations and that observation set the stage for more potential reflection and subsequent actions on Julie's part. If principals and assistant principals are willing to take this side-door approach to improvement by building trust, providing resources, and encouraging experimentation, then the school can begin to move forward without the benefit of a pep rally, stage lights, or rousing marches by John Philip Sousa. If Julie's assistant principal continues to support her as she makes changes and experiments with process and content methodology, that developing and supportive relationship will accelerate growth on her part.

Building administrators can also begin to improve customer service, refine or replace critical processes, and foster employee-to-employee relationships by working tirelessly with individuals and small groups within the school. If processes are identified for improvement, process-improvement teams can be set up to tackle the problem. Small grade-level groups can work on issues related to that grade level, and vertical teams can work across grade levels. Solving a process-related problem in the bus loop can be handled by a small team of those closest to the problem. It is hardly necessary, however, for teams to meet on every single improvement piece in the building. It is important for every school employee to understand that there is no existing process that can't be improved, there is no classroom where progress can't be made, and there is no one who should be satisfied with the status quo.

Final Thoughts

It would be great if the culture in every school was one of optimism and continual experimentation. It would be wonderful if every school viewed itself as a dynamic organization committed to change in the name of continuous improvement. The fact that this may not be so in every case should not keep teachers, grade-level groups, department-level teams, cafeteria supervisors and workers, custodial employees, and front office staff members from seeking to make what they do better. This involves taking risks, but taking risks on behalf of kids is a good thing.

In the final chapter, Chapter 8, we'll explore some ways to get started on the continuous-improvement highway.

8

Asking Questions and Getting Started

In his bestselling book, *Good to Great*, Jim Collins (2001) tells us that "good is the enemy of great" (p. 1). We as humans have become satisfied with companies, educational systems, and lives that are simply good; what is good is often acceptable. If the leaders in the building and the leaders in the classroom think that things seem to be fine as they are, they are not asking enough questions or questioning enough answers. Leadership, says Collins, is in part "about creating a climate where the truth is heard and the brutal facts confronted" (p. 74). Leadership is not so much about having a briefcase full of answers as it is about asking "questions that will lead to the best possible insights" (p. 75). Good leaders and good organizations question everything in a never-ending search for ways to improve.

I believe this is what administrators, supervisors, teachers, para-professionals, cafeteria workers, and students need to begin doing as a way of breaking out of this things-seem-fine-as-they-are or pretty-good-is-acceptable way of thinking. The biggest obstacle to improvement is not external. The tough, leathery skin of complacency is what holds schools back. It is easy to play the blame game, as we saw earlier, and use external barriers (real or imaginable) as excuses to march in place, measuring little in the way of forward progress. Getting onto the continuous-improvement highway in the first place requires that people start asking questions about *how* and *what* they are doing on a daily basis.

Appendices A and C of this book list processes that combine to form the system under which the school is operating at any given time, both inside and outside the classrooms. These processes need to be challenged by asking questions. For example, what follows is a series of questions related to the functioning of the cafeteria in every school. A small team of stakeholders might do well to spend some time reflecting on the processes explicit or implicit in these questions:

- To what extent does the quality of the food served in the cafeteria contribute to the health of the students and adults who consume it on a daily basis? What does the existing research on nutrition say about what is served and what could be served? Are there school districts in this state, country, or elsewhere that have tackled this issue of supporting the health of students through a balance between cost and quality? If so, can we visit those districts or schools? Can we at least get them involved in a conference call?
- What is the process by which students enter and leave the cafeteria? Would observing that process for a week while taking notes raise more questions and highlight possible problems or inefficiencies?
- What placement of cafeteria furniture (tables, chairs, trash cans, condiment tables) might result in a more efficient overall system that has the happy effect of eliminating confusion, reducing the amount of heavy traffic and noise, and decreasing confrontations?
- Would the playing of classical music or soft jazz contribute to a calm environment? Can we call around to see if anyone else is doing this? Is there some research that supports this?
- Is the amount of time students wait in order to get into the serving lines contributing to discipline problems? If so, how could we reduce the wait time?
- Is customer-service training provided on a regular basis for cafeteria supervisors and employees? If not, is it desirable to do that at the district level? If the district is not willing to provide such training, is there a way it can be provided at the school level?
- Are cafeteria employees who serve food or work at the point of sale establishing relationships with students? Internally, are

cafeteria staff members regularly establishing working relationships with the adults whom they serve?

- If the floor and the tables are a mess when students leave, what could be done to fix that not just temporarily but permanently? (I have been in spotless cafeterias that remain so through multiple lunch bells, and I have been in cafeterias where one has to look down to avoid slipping on milk cartons, food, or plastic forks and spoons.)
- Does whatever cafeteria supervision process we are using contribute to the smooth running of the system in place? Is it more effective during one lunch bell than another? If so, what are the variables that contribute to the relative success in that lunch bell? (I was in one cafeteria where the supervisor was taking notes related to process, to be used later on to improve the experience for students and adult employees alike.)

Often, parents and community members volunteer to be part of the supervision system in effect in the cafeteria. It has been my experience that these well-meaning and truly caring individuals last only a few days, sometimes only a few hours, before they leave, never to return. In many cases, those volunteers find themselves trying to function effectively in a system that is broken. There may be little training for such volunteers on how to function effectively with a large room full of hundreds of students. There may be little effort to provide for self-governance and self-evaluation among the student population using the lunchroom, the lack of which effectively hands the entire burden for discipline and control over to a few supervisors, including those well-meaning parents or senior citizens. This begs the final, and most important, question facing any team charged with improving things during lunch: *If the processes that make up the system are broken, how can they be improved or replaced to make the lunch environment one that will consistently support and serve students, teachers, administrators, volunteers, and visitors?*

Teachers Questioning Everything

Teachers who are desirous of change and interested in serious systemic improvement will find it necessary to take a close look at process and ask a few questions of their own:

- How do I deliver content? How do my students *react* to how I deliver content? How could I get feedback from them on a regular basis as to how they feel about how I deliver content?
- Do I spend time developing powerful relationships with students and parents? Do I spend time working with students on improving their own student-to-student relationships in my classroom? Is there a way to measure the effectiveness of my efforts at relationship building?
- Am I doing most of the talking in my classroom, or do I get my students involved in face-to-face discussions with each other in pairs or groups? If I tried that and there were problems, how could I determine what caused the problems, and could I enlist the support of the students to improve the whole student-to-student conversation process?
- Do I change gears in class every few minutes? If I don't, is it possible my students and I are paying a price for that? If my habit is to have my ninth graders sit still for most of a ninety-minute block, what do they think of that? If I experimented with changing gears every ten minutes or so in a particular block, what did they think of that? If it did not run as smoothly as I had hoped, why was that so? Can I enlist the help of my students to adjust or improve the processes used during that block?
- Is there research that shows that tracking progress over time is beneficial to the continuous-improvement process of individual students and the class as a whole? If so, what mechanisms could I put in place to track student progress over time, collectively and individually? Would the development of student portfolios assist students and parents as they try to visualize student progress over time?
- Do I allow enough time for student reflection and information processing individually, in pairs, or in groups? Is there research that supports providing gobs of time for reflection and processing? Once I have my students processing information in pairs or groups, can I have them self-evaluate how they did using a checklist or rubric on listening or speaking skills?
- Are the transitions from seatwork to feetwork (standing paired conversations or charting, for example) smooth and quick? If they were, would it save that most important ingredient—time?
- If I am working with a group of six or seven students on reading, what are the other students in my classroom doing? Are they engaged? Are they being productive?

- Do I allow enough time after asking a question so that students can think and then formulate an answer? Is there some research that shows that wait time is important?
- Do I have other teachers visit my classroom in an attempt to get feedback from them on how I am doing as it relates to management, delivery, timing, presentation skills, and anything else related to instruction? (I recommend that teachers have colleagues visit and look for one or two things only during the observation. For example, have them watch the students and look for signs of engagement. Have them observe you and determine if you allow enough wait time after asking a question. Ask them to observe anything related to time management. Keep it simple but keep the observations coming.)
- Is there a professional-development library in my school? If so, where is it located and who is in charge? Would setting aside thirty minutes a week to do nothing but read educational journals and books related to instruction accelerate my own continuous-improvement journey? (It would!)

These are all process-related issues and need to be dealt with regardless of the course content. Teachers should be in a constant search (individually and collectively with colleagues) for possible research that will inform their own decisions. The overall instructional system in place in any classroom is only as good as the individual processes that make up that system. If it is obvious to teachers that something is consistently not working, they must find time to search for root causes and solutions.

For example, if the amount of completed homework in a middle school math class is steadily declining as the weeks go by in September, what are the root causes of that decline? Faced with a declining rate of returned assignments, some teachers will simply shrug their shoulders and say, "My goodness, these kids today are lazier than in my day!" This is an excuse that does nothing to discover the underlying causes of a decline in the amount of homework. I once observed a middle school social studies teacher, Scott McKenzie, who actually charted the rate of homework return on a bar graph over the course of several weeks in the fall. The visual provided by this graph made him sit up and take notice. He knew the rate of return was declining, but the visual told him that the rate of decline was bad and getting worse week by week.

McKenzie then gave his students a two-week moratorium on homework, and then he began asking questions of his students directly related to why the rate of return was declining—after all, it was they who were not completing the assignments—then he actually charted the results. It appeared that there were some reasons that were more important, or appeared more frequently, and one of them was that students simply forgot or did not bother to write down the assignments, or for whatever reason they simply did not make time in the evening to complete the assignments.

In addition to charting the rate of return for homework, McKenzie also kept a chart showing the grade average for each of his four classes. He then put both charts on different transparencies, turned on the overhead, and juxtaposed the charts. This new visual showed a correlation between the amount of homework returned and the grades for tests and quizzes. He then asked them what they noticed about the two sets of results as indicated on the two charts. What became apparent to them was that when they took the time to do their homework, grades increased. When the homework declined, so did the grades.

Having identified several reasons why the homework was no longer coming in, and after taking the time to look at the correlation between homework and grades, McKenzie and his students spent a little time each day coming up with a plan that included adjustments (fewer assignments, but more feedback, and a quicker return from teacher to students, for example). With questions asked, input received, and adjustments promised, McKenzie began to give homework assignments once more. He continued to chart his rate of return, and for the rest of the semester the rate stayed high—and the grades went up.

The key here is that this teacher was willing to do several things in pursuit of continuous improvement:

1. He acknowledged to himself and to the students that the homework system as it was currently being administered was not working.

2. He made the decision to halt what seemed to be a dysfunctional system until he could get at the reasons why the return rate was declining.

3. Instead of blaming his students, or berating them, or telling them he used to walk to school barefoot in zero-degree weather and six feet of snow, he actually sought their input and, by so doing, surfaced some interesting root causes for the homework not coming in.

4. Working with the students, he came up with a new system composed of several improved processes. The overall system was improved by examining the attendant processes and making whatever adjustments were necessary.

The students, by the way, appreciated the teacher's willingness to open up, admit to his own shortcomings, and solicit their help in the continuous-improvement process (McKenzie, 1995; personal communication, December 15, 2010).

The First Place Everyone Goes

In schools committed to continuous improvement, no one in the school community is exempt from the commitment. Administrators, teachers, paraprofessionals, support staff, and students are all capable of moving down the continuous-improvement highway. No system that relates to human resources, physical plant, classroom effectiveness, transportation, student diet, or anything else connected to school should be exempt from an ongoing commitment to continuous improvement, and that includes the front office; everyone who visits the school begins there. Every quality organization understands the importance of first impressions. A bad first impression on the part of anyone in the organization can impede forward progress considerably, and those in the front office are on the front line every day.

I love walking into the front office of a school, and over the course of four decades in education and educational sales, I have been in hundreds of front offices in several states. In many of those office visits, I have been greeted by someone immediately on coming through the door. That person stands up, smiles, looks me in the eye, approaches me at the counter, and gives me the impression that I am now the center of focus until we do what we need to do, or until she takes me to the person I need to see.

There are times when I have been ignored on entering the office. I have been in front offices where as many as three employees behind the counter make me wait for up to a minute before one of them even acknowledges I'm there. All the efforts going on in the name of continuous improvement throughout the building will be adversely affected by the community's perception that this school seems not to care about those who come to visit or do business there. I often consider that it costs little to greet visitors quickly, pleasantly, and efficiently. It costs a *great deal* to allow situations where visitor after visitor goes away bewildered, reflecting on the way to their cars that the school that is tasked with serving their children serves adults so poorly.

In these safety-conscious times, the first contact may come with someone sitting at a desk in the hallway *outside* the office. Once again, one of two things invariably happens with that first contact: The visitor either *feels welcome* or *does not feel welcome* in the building. One or the other. The first impression is either good or bad, and for a parent or anyone else who has business in the school, this first contact is critical to how she views the school. In the face of a bad first impression, the second point of contact in the building has to work hard to turn that visitor's frown into a smile. After being warmly greeted by a volunteer just inside the front entrance to an elementary school, I mentioned this to the principal. She said she looked long and hard for volunteers who could, scores of times during the school day, make visitors feel consistently welcome and valued.

First impressions being what they are, schools and districts must make customer service a priority. The training should include a facilitated session where employees reflect on how important first impressions are to those who choose to walk through the front door of the school, no matter the reason for their visit. Because everyone in the building is impacted by the power of these first impressions, segments of the entire school population should be included. During this session, stakeholders (employees, students, parents) can reflect while working in small groups on what *they* feel like in the face of both poor and exemplary customer service. Under the facilitation of someone who is able to keep everyone focused, the group can work to flesh out answers to the following questions:

- What constitutes good customer service?
- What constitutes *excellent* customer service?
- Who are our customers, internal and external?
- Why are good first impressions important?
- Why is follow-up important? (By this I mean why is it important for an office employee to make certain the customer is firmly reconnected with someone before he disconnects? I recommend that whenever it is possible for an office worker to physically accompany the visitor to the next point of contact, she should do so.)
- Why is *consistently* excellent customer service critical to the improvement process *in this building?* What training would

improve customer service and efficiency in the front office? If the district does not provide such training, are there professional-development funds available at the district or building level that would allow front-office personnel to attend a one- or two-day customer-service seminar? (Before sending personnel to these seminars, check them out. Get references and talk to people who have attended them, and then follow up with those among your employees who attended in order to make certain that what was learned gets institutionalized. The follow-up is critical; otherwise those who participated in the seminar or workshop may simply return to the status quo, and what could have been powerful is less so.)

First Responders

Two questions are critical when it comes to first impressions in the front office of a school:

- When the phone rings, what happens? Who does what and how quickly?
- When someone walks in the front door, what happens if the only office professional present is on the phone?
- What is good phone etiquette, and do we provide training for office professionals related to answering the phone and talking with customers?
- If we have a machine answering the phone, would our customers be better served by replacing that system with a live, pleasant office professional?

In the name of "efficiency," school districts all over the country have replaced a human being with an electronic voice. Interestingly, during scores of customer-service training sessions with thousands of school employees over the years, I always asked one question during the workshop: How many of you prefer to hear the voice of a real person when you call a company? In every case, nearly 100 percent of these school employees said they preferred the human touch rather than the electronic voice and punching numbers on keypads in an attempt to talk with someone at the company. Nearly 100 percent every time. There is no more important first-impression issue than who (a person) or what (a machine) answers the phone. I love it when someone actually answers the phone in a school office, and I feel great when that person smiles over the phone and then *truly listens*. This is no small thing. Whether it is on the phone or at the counter, first impressions are critical.

When teams of employees meet to answer the questions we have been asking, it is helpful if there is a process facilitator in the room whose job it is to maximize efficiency, get everyone to share, come to a consensus on key issues, come up with a product, and work with administrators to make certain there is follow through. The process facilitator may be a school- or district-level employee, or if there is no one in house who can handle this important function, it may mean bringing in someone from outside the school community, someone who is truly seen as not having a stake in the ultimate outcomes. This person should be dedicated to surfacing possible barriers to progress and then leading the group toward removing those barriers on the way to arriving at a final solution that has the support of all stakeholders. Not every team needs a facilitator to function, but there must be a set of norms that guide the team during meetings. Also—and this is critical—the team must know exactly *why* they have been brought together. Nothing is more frustrating than thinking you are there to make a decision and then finding out your task was simply to provide some input for the decision maker. Everyone must know exactly what is expected, and when what is expected is due.

The Improvement Spiral

During my early years as a teacher, I answered the question, "Is what I am doing working?" in a very teacher-centered way. My goal was to control my ninth graders, keeping them seated and quietly industrious. I did the talking; they did the listening (meaning they smiled at me while going to a better place in their minds) and the note taking. My students thoughtfully provided me with quiz and test grades for my grade book, and everything unfolded according to plan. My students survived ninth-grade U.S. History, and I learned a great deal about the subject—my students, perhaps, not so much.

The Plan–Do–Study–Act (PDSA) cycle was unknown to me at the time. In typical 20/20 hindsight, I now understand that I was caught in the "do" part of that cycle and did not spend a lot of time evaluating how I did what I did. Because my classroom was decidedly teacher centered, and because what I was doing worked for me, I would have said, "It's working!" Whether it is working for

Figure 8.1   Continuous-Improvement Cycle (PDSA)

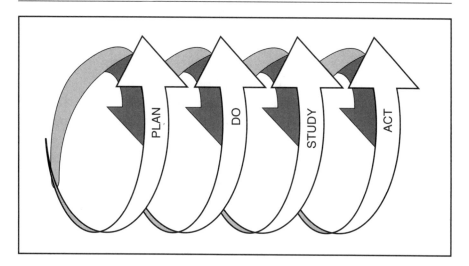

Source: Nash (2010). Created by Dianne Kinnison.

me is not as important as whether it is working for the students, and knowing that involves a good deal of self-reflection and self-evaluation. Getting better over time means planning what one is going to do, doing it, evaluating it, and making necessary adjustments. The cycle is not a closed one; it spirals out until the teacher or school employee retires. There is no end in sight, for the simple reason that there is no real finish line. Figure 8.1 represents this continuous-improvement spiral.

The keys to continuous improvement lie in a willingness to hold what you are doing up to the light and then to take the time to determine its effectiveness. Everyone *in* the organization should continually be evaluating his or her impact *on* the organization. For teachers, the word "working" in the question, "Is what I'm currently doing working?" has to be defined in terms of student progress. Just as teacher mentors are dedicated to the professional growth of teachers, teachers are dedicated to the academic growth of students. When a classroom is teacher centered, success may be defined in terms of comfortable routines and a very satisfying status quo that has been developed and refined over the years. As it was with me early in my teaching career, teachers and other school employees may get stuck in the "do" phase of the PDSA cycle (Figure 8.2); at this point it becomes a continuous loop, rather than a spiral, and the employee simply settles in for the long haul.

Figure 8.2   PDSA Cycle
(Continuous Loop)

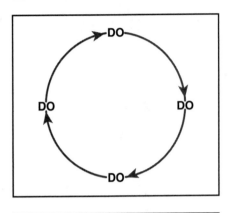

Source: Nash (2010). Created by Dianne Kinnison.

The only way to move forward in any meaningful and consistent way is to change something; otherwise, we are in neutral. Let's look at an example of the PDSA cycle in action. Mrs. Slattery, a middle school language arts teacher, has her eighth graders write multiparagraph essays during the course of the school year. The state writing tests given in March have showed uneven results for her students over the past two years, and she is in her classroom the week after the students have gone home for the summer. We'll join her as she picks up with the evaluation, or study, phase of PDSA.

Study. Looking at a sampling of student essays, Mrs. Slattery notices several points of weakness, not the least of which is in the area of grammar and sentence structure. After two years of disappointing test results, she is no longer willing to proceed with business as usual. Instead of doing what many of her teacher friends do (play the blame game for poor results), she decides to make some changes in the way she teaches writing.

Act. Looking at her school district's professional-development course offerings, she found a five-hour workshop related to writing and signed up. The workshop facilitator modeled something called Edit Doctor, where the workshop participants worked together to "fix patients" (the patients were all essays in need of grammatical help). Mrs. Slattery was impressed and spoke with other teachers who had experienced great success with this strategy. She also decided to include a student checklist based on her own teacher checklist, developed from the state English standards. This would allow students to see if they had checked for grammar, topic sentences, and other components of a good multiparagraph essay. She also decided to give students a lot more written feedback on their essay drafts during the school year.

Plan. Later in the summer, after everything was developed, she posted the checklist on her teacher website, with an explanation for parents interested in helping their kids in the writing process. She developed several different essays for the Edit

Doctor segments, with transparencies that her eighth graders could look at in order to check their own work after each group fixed its patient. She planned a process whereby she could sample essays—a necessary step because she was going to have them write more of them—in order to provide more written feedback on a regular basis. Having read an article on formative assessments, Mrs. Slattery decided to increase the number of student essays, while providing tons of written feedback, but fewer actual grades. She also planned to involve her students in a formative peer-review process.

Do. Mrs. Slattery put this new system in place in September, and the students took part in their initial Edit Doctor activity during the first week of school. She also had them read several excellent essays, allowing them to pass them from student to student in the course of fifteen minutes. At the end of that time, she had them stand and break into groups of three or four, discussing among themselves why the essays they had read were indeed excellent pieces of writing. While they talked, she circulated around the room, listening carefully to the various conversations. Based on what she overheard, she then led a class discussion on various points. Using the sampling process and some peer review to provide plenty of written feedback on an ongoing basis, their first essay drafts became final drafts by the end of the third week of September.

Study. Rather than wait until the following June to evaluate what they had done with an eye toward her own instructional practices, Mrs. Slattery spent one Saturday morning looking over the essays, comparing them to last year's efforts. What she discovered was that the grammar had improved, something that made her feel good. She also called a few parents that Saturday morning in order to compliment them on the essays their students had written. What she discovered, along with their appreciation for the calls, was that a couple of them had actually gone to her website and used the checklist she had posted there in order to see that all the components were there.

Act. She made the decision to continue Edit Doctor and revisit the checklists with her students from time to time. Also, she noticed that the overall quality of the essays was okay but would need to be much better. Before lunch on that Saturday morning, Mrs. Slattery decided to look around for, or compose, a writing rubric with a four- or five-point scale that would help her students to be more self-directed.

Plan.   The next week, Mrs. Slattery talked with another eighth-grade English teacher, to discover that she used a simple, but effective, four-point rubric for her own students. She was willing to share the rubric, and Mrs. Slattery introduced it to her students that week, posting it on her website. She made it a point to call the two parents who had utilized the checklist to let them know that this additional self-assessment tool was now available.

Do.   By October, the new four-point rubric had joined the checklist, Edit Doctor, and feedback sampling as valuable tools in Mrs. Slattery's arsenal. She put everything in play and collected some newly completed essays at the end of October. She also used those few weeks to call even more parents, telling them about what was available on her website that could benefit their eighth graders. To make sure they knew how to use the rubric, she worked with the class to score an essay that was projected onto the screen. She then gave pairs of students an unidentified essay (from a previous year), asking them to see if they could score the essay working together with a copy of the rubric in front of them.

Study.   On a late October Tuesday, after school, Mrs. Slattery went through this new batch of essays, discovering once again that her students were improving. She also noticed something else: The amount of corrective feedback she was giving students was less than on the first batch. She realized this was for the simple reason that they were making fewer errors. Also, the peer-editing process worked to assist the student whose essay was being edited, along with the one doing the editing. It now took her less time to provide feedback on the essays, and she spent the next couple of days giving feedback to all ninety-seven students. On many of the essays, the amount of corrective feedback Mrs. Slattery had to provide was limited to a couple of minor comments. Over the first two months of school, her students' ability to write persuasive and informational essays was at a level that exceeded what last year's students had been able to do in the spring.

What Mrs. Slattery began to realize during the course of this exercise in continuous improvement was that the strategies she had employed over those two months had worked as accelerants to progress. She had no doubt that by March her students would be more than ready to take the state exams. What really astonished her was that her eighth graders actually enjoyed grammar because of the way she approached it. She went to her file drawers and discarded all her old worksheets and began to develop some new Edit Doctor "patients." She shared them with the teacher who had given her the writing rubric, and at the next faculty meeting, they both shared what worked for them with the faculty. The social studies teacher on Mrs. Slattery's eight-grade team developed his own Edit Doctor essays by writing short, lively biographies of less-than-famous, but nevertheless interesting, Americans. The social studies teacher also decided to use the writing rubric for multiparagraph essays and introduced a number of formative essays into his program.

Getting Started on "Go!"

For teachers who want to take the on-ramp onto the continuous-improvement highway, here are some ways to get started:

1. Meet with the principal or the assistant principal with whom you normally work and tell that administrator that you are going to be taking a close look at the way you teach. She may be able to generate some ideas with you, and you may want to ask if it is possible for her to provide a substitute teacher so you can visit the classroom of someone in the district who pursues and uses best practices. In the prologue of this book, it was the assistant principal who arranged for Julie to visit the classroom of an excellent teacher in another school.

2. Find out if your school's media center has a professional-development library; if so, take a trip down there and spend a day during the summer looking over articles and books on continuous improvement, formative assessment, managing process in classrooms, and brain-based learning. Related to this last topic, invest some time researching how the brain works. This is critical to processes related to teaching and learning. If you can afford it, I would suggest you subscribe to an educational journal dedicated to best practices and educational progress, such as *Ed Leadership* (ASCD).

3. Find another teacher or group of teachers, and begin a regular series of conversations about what works and what does not work as it relates to student progress—not as it relates to the relative comfort of the status quo. Getting on the continuous-improvement highway means you are going to need to leave the status quo in the dust. If you are working with some other teachers, perhaps in grade-level teams, arrange to visit each other's classrooms. Here are some "look fors" when you are observing:

   o Who seems to be doing the most work—students or teacher?
   o Do students seem to be engaged in the learning?
   o What do the body language and facial expressions of the students say about their involvement in what is going on in the classroom?
   o When the teacher asks a question, does she allow three to five seconds of wait time before responding, allowing students time to think?
   o Are the students seated for the duration of your visit, or does the teacher provide opportunities for them to get up and move?
   o Are students provided with opportunities to reflect and process information?
   o Does the teacher get students up, moving, and discussing content in pairs, trios, or quartets?
   o Is the classroom set up to allow for student movement and interaction?
   o Is the classroom free of sarcasm (anyone's) and disrespect?
   o Do processes seem to flow smoothly (getting the class period started, distribution of handouts, purposeful movement, transitioning from one activity to another)?
   o Are directions clear, and are they given one at a time?

4. If you have someone visit your classroom, ask them to look for certain things, perhaps related to two or three of the preceding "look fors." After the observation, find the time to talk and reflect with the teacher or administrator who did the observing. Look for ways to improve every process you manage in the classroom. In doing that, you are finding ways to connect with kids, engage them in meaningful learning, save time, and avoid rabbit trails that will disrupt the instructional flow and tempo.

5. Take a close look at the standards that guide your instruction. Is what you are doing aligned to those standards? If you are

using checklists and rubrics, are they closely tied to the standards? Can you identify some neat stuff you have used for many years that really does not contribute to the overall improvement process as it relates to the standards in your content area? You have to be willing to jettison some things that do not contribute to the continuous-improvement journey of the students in your care. This is sometimes tough to do; it may be that the kids love it, but time is precious and should not be wasted.

6. Communication (oral and written), critical thinking, and problem solving are all critical components in the global economy your students will become part of when they graduate. Do the activities and strategies you employ assist students in these areas? When you put a picture or other graphic on the screen, do you simply explain what you and they are seeing, or do you let them explain to each other in pairs or groups what they think they see? Do you encourage them to ask questions, rather than simply searching for the right answers? If you are a science teacher, are you willing to use that checklist and rubric when your kids write? Every student at every level needs to be given time to think, ponder, reflect, question, explain, illustrate, summarize, infer, analyze, and synthesize. This means turning over the workload to the students. They should be doing 80 percent of the work, not the other way around. Discuss these concepts with other teachers at your grade level or in your department, or even with those in other grade levels or departments. The math teacher who has powerful process-management skills has much to discuss and share with a social studies teacher who is strong in other areas.

7. See if you and your friends can convince your school's leadership team to replace faculty meetings devoted to "administrivia" with learning opportunities for teachers who can use that time to look collectively at assessment data or to work on process- or content-related issues common to everyone in the building (from noisy hallways to enlisting everyone in improving reading scores).

8. Shift your assessment from the summative side to the formative side and commit to giving your students feedback that is meaningful, timely, and corrective in nature. The goal here is not to collect grades but to accelerate student progress.

Students can keep portfolios showing their own progress over time, and you can take the time to sit down with students as frequently as time permits in order to listen to them and provide more feedback.

9. Have students use run charts or bar graphs to plot their own progress over time. I know teachers who use such graphics to show collective improvement for classes or grade levels. All these charts provide teachers with talking points when meeting with parents. They need feedback, too, and "Your son is doing really well!" does not help them understand where, along a continuum, Eddie is currently positioned in his continuous-improvement journey. Looking at Eddie's run chart, for example, as it relates to his progress in writing, gives teachers an opportunity to explain the rubric that forms the basis for the measurement. It is specific and understandable, and I have found that this clarity makes for a much more substantive conversation with parents.

10. Don't keep anything related to process a secret from students. Show them the spiral graphic (Figure 8.1) and let them discuss with each other, in pairs or trios, how they think it might relate to continuous improvement. Then, have them ask questions of you, the answers to which may illuminate for them how important the improvement cycle is. Then, relate it to something specific: writing essays, solving math problems, improving reading scores, improving processes in the gym during PE, their own health, or anything else related to your course or their lives.

Your students rely on you to put in place a system that will accelerate *their* progress. This means teachers must invest time in putting how they do what they do under the microscope on a regular basis. Plan what you are going to do, do it, evaluate it, make adjustments, and move on. I have already pointed out that, early in my career as a teacher, I did not do this. I did not come close to doing this. I *did* learn a great deal about the history of the United States but only *because I did most of the work in my classes*. A learner-centered classroom is one in which teaching processes (lecture, teacher talk) are replaced by learning processes (student reflection and engagement, cognitive strategies, student-to-student interaction).

Above all, perhaps, teachers need to create classrooms where students see themselves as full-time participants and active contributors to their own continuous-improvement journeys. Short-, medium-, and long-term goals will provide signposts along the way, and those goals are most powerful when they are decided upon by the students themselves. According to Lipton and Wellman (2000), "Learning is a goal-driven activity. When learners feel like they own these goals, motivation and enthusiasm increase" (p. 8). This process is facilitated, affirm Lipton and Wellman, "through modeling, mediating, and reflecting on both the learning in process and on the processes of learning" (p. 8). When teachers get caught in a circular "do" cycle, without the deep reflection and honest examination that accompanies a meaningful evaluation of how teachers do what they do—and how students do what they do—then everyone is caught on a treadmill that goes nowhere.

Final Thoughts

Administrators and teachers must create a culture of optimism where negativity and the "negaholics" who practice such behavior are not welcome, and where pessimism is shown the door. The spirit of continuous improvement is one of experimentation and risk taking on behalf of kids; it involves a willingness to reflect on the totality of what goes on in the classroom and not to shy away from the brutal facts. The spirit of improvement is transparent—there is little or nothing that can't be shared, discussed, and reflected upon with the students. They need to understand how the improvement cycle (PDSA) works and why their progress depends on working smarter and harder along the way. If the commitment to continuous improvement is not rock solid, students will find the path of least resistance, and this applies to teachers as well. Getting better should not be optional, and it will be rewarding for those who truly commit to the journey.

The best building principals I know simply refuse to allow the status quo to go unchallenged, and the same is true of the best teachers. Excellent principals and teachers understand that if everything seems okay, they are not asking enough questions or questioning enough answers. The students in our care need us to facilitate and accelerate their journey down the continuous-improvement highway. They need us to model the kind of process improvement that will improve systems; it is necessary for us to take the long view when searching for ways to make progress on many fronts in the schoolhouse. Everything from the front office to the classroom should be open to examination and improvement. Every mind should be open to change, and taking risks on behalf of students amounts to noble acts that ultimately help them meet and exceed expectations—their own and those of the adults entrusted with their education.

In the Epilogue, we'll join our fictional middle school teacher, Julie, who is about to make a phone call that will hugely and positively impact her professional life.

Epilogue

Julie and her Falcon Team colleagues had some cake in Julie's classroom after lunch. Before everyone returned to his or her own room to begin the paperwork necessary to check out the next day, they all congratulated the math teacher on his retirement. While she certainly did not wish him ill, Julie was glad to see him go. His constant negativity was a drain on them all, and it was a sore spot for their hundred-plus seventh graders as well. He spoke of moving back to his boyhood home in Ohio, and they all took part in a good deal of small talk until about 2:15, when her teammates left, allowing Julie to do some more thinking about how she was going to make some improvements in her own instructional methodology.

Late that afternoon, Julie called Lisa, the social studies teacher whom she had observed in late March and invited her to lunch the following week. Lisa agreed, and the two of them met at a local restaurant that next Tuesday at noon. They ordered, chatted for a while, and then Julie explained to Lisa that she was beginning to have doubts about her ability to connect with her seventh graders and then involve them more directly in their own learning. She told Lisa that her main mode of delivery was lecture, with a few videos and worksheets sprinkled in for good measure. Lisa listened intently, and when their food came, both were quiet for a couple of minutes.

"How many years have you taught, Lisa?" asked Julie.

"This was my seventh year in teaching, and the fourth in the school where you observed me in the spring," Lisa replied. "At the end of the third year at my old school, I felt much the same way as you do now. My answer to my dilemma was simply to move to a new middle school when the opportunity arose."

"Did the move help?" asked Julie.

Lisa laughed and said, "No, not really. I'm afraid I had played the blame game enough in that first school to believe that my lack of success really had little to do with me. I was in a lunch group with friends who spent a good deal of time complaining, and I complained as much as anyone. No, the move to another middle school did not automatically solve anything, but there was something in place at the new school that had not existed in the first."

Lisa paused, took a sip of her iced tea, and continued. "My teammates at the new middle school are great, but there was something begun by a former principal that made a big difference as far as ramping up my own improvement efforts."

Lisa took a bite of her hamburger, looked out the window for a few moments, and went on with her story. "Years ago, the administration in this school insisted that teachers in the same subject area meet with the other three teachers at their respective grade levels. There was not much in the way of clear direction as to what should be accomplished at these regular meetings, and as the years went by, the meetings became less frequent—except for the four seventh-grade social studies teachers."

In order to give Lisa some time to eat, rather than talk while her food got cold, Julie interrupted, "My own Falcon Team colleagues are good friends, and we meet twice per week, but we don't really focus on instruction. I'm afraid we spend too much time playing that blame game you spoke of. Some of those meetings are downers, to be honest. Also, none of the subject-area teachers meet at any level, to my knowledge, although I can't be sure of that. What makes your meetings with the other social studies teachers different?"

Lisa smiled and said, "It is the most amazing group, and our meetings are not only consistently positive but highly productive as well. Over the last four years, each of us has been able to attend workshops from which we are able to bring back specific classroom strategies, many of them related to formative assessments, and that has made all the difference. There was money to go to these workshops, but no one else really wanted to go, so each year at least one of us on our team took advantage of this and went."

"You mentioned in March that you look at assessment data on a regular basis," said Julie. "How does that work?"

"Well," replied Lisa, "we, the social studies teachers, that is, have developed common assessments based on the state standards. We schedule those exams throughout the year so that we can compare notes in terms of how well our students did. If we find that one teacher did a particularly good job of teaching the Civil War, for example, then we take a close look at that teacher's methodology in the weeks prior to the exam. Also, our administration provides covers on occasion, so that we can observe each other in action. I can honestly say, Julie, that I have learned more about teaching in these four years than I did in the previous eleven, and that includes four years of college. Each of us has strengths, and those common assessments revealed them. It was an eye opener for me, and it made me understand how much seeing other people teach can provide for someone, like you, actually, who is willing to examine how she does what she does in the classroom."

"I see what you mean, and it must be powerful for your social studies teammates," replied Julie.

Lisa nodded. "The four of us have an intense passion about our nation's history, and not a day goes by that we don't explore delivery methods that stand a chance of improving our instruction. We have a seventh-grade history website that includes a common checklist and rubric for writing. Every seventh-grade student has access to the site, and it includes samples of essays and other examples of written pieces that help them understand the rubric. The parents love it, too, and the written work in these history classes has improved steadily over the years. We find that the kids use the checklist and rubric in their other classes as well."

"Wow, Lisa," said Julie. "It sounds like you have your act together."

"I guess we do, but keep in mind that all this has been four years in the making. We have tried to get the current administrators to help us spread the word, but the truth is that many teachers don't want to put in the hours and the planning we do. The performance of our seventh graders on the state exams is consistently high, and they do beautifully in their state writing exams as well."

Lisa paused, finished her iced tea, and continued, "Two points I want to make about all this. First, the support from parents is amazing. They love the website and they love the fact that their kids are doing so well. Second, those three other social studies teachers and I are in constant continuous-improvement mode. One success leads to another, and we are not afraid to try anything that we think might benefit our kids."

"I may look into doing that at our school," said Julie. "I know the other two social studies teachers but only slightly. We don't meet professionally at all."

They finished their meals in silence and declined dessert. The check appeared, and Julie gave her credit card to the waitress. She told Lisa that it was she who had invited her, and the visit had been worth it.

Lisa thanked her and said, "Here is the great thing about all this, Julie. The four of us no longer play the blame game. If something is not working, we fix it or discard it outright. We have gotten rid of most of our worksheets, and we follow any video segment—and they are short—with paired or group discussions on what they just saw, or with a few minutes for reflecting in their journals. We have our students communicating and processing often with various partners or trios. We actually cover less material than we all used to, but we go more deeply into what we *do* cover. We are not satisfied unless the students are truly engaged. We give written feedback on homework, but we give less homework. It's that whole quality over quantity thing, I guess. We are on an improvement journey that we understand will never end. We just keep taking risks on behalf of the kids, and it results in a better performance effort on both our part and theirs. It is time consuming, but it is fun and satisfying."

Having settled with the waitress, they stood to leave. On their way to the parking lot, Julie said, "I'm not sure where to start here, Lisa. This is all new territory for me, and our administration has not really launched any top-down improvement initiative that I can think of."

"Here is your first task, and I'm going to say this because I think you are where I was a few short years ago, and there is an urgency in your voice that you can turn to your advantage," said Lisa. "Decide right now that you are going to turn the corner on this. Decide right now that regardless of the support you do or don't get from your leadership team, you will work to improve *how* you do *what* you do. I spent my first three years of teaching in neutral, not going anywhere. It was not until I got to the new school that I realized it didn't have to be like that. You don't have to change schools, Julie, to come to that conclusion or to turn that corner."

"It should help that we have a negative teacher on our team who is leaving," said Julie. "He was a master at the blame game, and I'm afraid we all did more than a bit of that over the past three years."

They got to Lisa's car, and she shook her head, saying, "Playing the blame game absolves you of doing anything. If everything is someone else's fault, then 'What can I do?' becomes a way to avoid getting started on your own program of improvement."

Lisa got into her car and rolled down the window. "Why don't you come to one of our summer meetings? The other seventh-grade social studies teachers get together three times during the summer months at my house." Lisa smiled, and added, "Did I tell you I have a pool? Anyway, we spend those meetings evaluating what we have done in the previous years. We read about new strategies we can incorporate into our programs, and we look at the feedback provided by the students in all four of our history classes. We get feedback from our students several times per year, and we process the feedback and make changes accordingly, if necessary."

Lisa suggested that Julie and her teammates visit the website she had referred to earlier and provided her with an e-mail address so they could stay in touch. Lisa was pleased that Julie had been so receptive and felt certain she would begin to make some changes, with or without other teachers at her middle school.

Julie took the card and said, "Thanks for having lunch with me, Lisa."

"Thanks for buying," said Lisa. She shook Julie's hand through the open window and started her car. "I know Terri Ann Lodge, one of the other seventh-grade social studies teachers at your school, and if you like, I'll call her and invite her to my house for that next meeting, which is two weeks from now."

"Let me call her first," said Julie, "and then you can extend the invitation. I want to explain to her what I'm trying to do. I also have a feeling I'll be working with my Falcon Team teammates to work on our own improvement plan. Becky and Yolanda are good friends and might be amenable to working with me."

Julie took out her keys, thanked Lisa once more, and headed for her car. She felt better than she had in months. Her March observation of Lisa's outstanding lesson, along with this extremely positive lunch meeting, gave her the inspiration to continue trying to get out of the rut she realized she had gotten herself into. Well, she mused, she was the one who put herself in the rut, and she would be the one to pull herself out. Having done that, she could start moving down a road that she was certain would benefit her and a new group of seventh graders. If she could do it with the help of her Falcon Team colleagues or the other two seventh-grade social studies teachers, so much the better, but she was committed to improving over time, regardless. Reaching her car, she opened the door, slid into the seat, started the engine—and smiled. She was doing something to shake herself out of her lethargy, and it felt good.

Appendix A

Processes Into Systems: Building Level

In organizations dedicated to continuous improvement as a way of life, there is nothing that is overlooked, from hiring processes to the process for getting feedback from those who leave the organization. There is nothing that cannot be improved, and it is necessary to identify specific areas of improvement and then to dedicate time, energy, and resources to make things run more smoothly and more efficiently. Processes that simply move along in deeply worn paths year after year will not help move the organization forward. Improving something requires an intervention of some sort; something that was not in place before must be put in place now, or the status quo will serve as a drag on forward movement.

Everything in the building should be seen as affecting instruction, although clearly instructional processes have a far more direct and immediate impact on learning. That said, as we saw in Chapter 3, a school climate that is conducive to change can serve as an accelerant to improvement. Stephanie Enzmann, currently an assistant principal at a middle school in Virginia, has served as a Baldrige Examiner and is uniquely qualified to identify and comment on several school-level processes that process-improvement teams could hold up to the light, examine, and seek to improve over time. We worked together to come up with a list of other-than-classroom issues that working teams can tackle on behalf of any school's continuous-improvement program.

Processes become systemic when a regular, effective program for their evaluation is implemented, with an eye toward improving virtually everything on the school campus, from the parking lot to the front office to the very floors everyone walks on every day. First on our list of processes that teams can visit and improve is the whole concept of first impressions; this includes the school's physical plant and the critical issue of customer service. First impressions are key components of well-run and inviting schools at any level.

First Impressions: Physical Plant

A study of twenty high-performing principals in high-performing or steadily improving schools conducted by Blase, Blase, and Phillips (2010) showed that "proper maintenance of the school plant was integral to teaching and learning." Furthermore, the appearance of their schools "was concretely and symbolically important to the public as well as to the staff, the teachers, and the students" (p. 56). According to those principals, the maintenance of their buildings is the responsibility of everyone in the school.

There are schools that are spotless, well lit, and beautifully maintained. This is a source of pride, I have found, and not only for the custodians; it takes a real collaborative effort to keep a building looking both inviting and safe. In other schools, I have seen paper in the hallways and I have observed marks on the walls that the simple and occasional touch-up of paint would eliminate. I recommend that a process-improvement team—with representatives of every employee group—create a working checklist that includes inspection points (locker repairs, marks on walls and floors, lights, windows, floors, desks and other furniture) that can be checked at least once per week.

Lighting, for example, is both an instructional and a safety issue; the use of the checklist means every teacher and employee in the building knows a process is in place—and is working—to ensure that the lighting fixtures are attended to as a matter of course. Otherwise, it remains for teachers to report that the light needs replaced; if that is not high on the list of priorities for that teacher, it may not be dealt with for many days or weeks. What is on the checklist is the result of an analysis of those things that not only make a good first impression but also contribute to the overall continuous-improvement effort in the building. Great teachers use checklists in their instruction; administrators can model their efficiency and utility by harnessing the power of checklists in the everyday operation of the building.

Also, when new custodians are hired, the building's head custodian should model for that new employee exactly what is expected. If, for example, there is a standard of cleanliness for floors, furniture, and walls in classrooms, the head custodian can work alongside the new employee, modeling exactly how meeting those standards should be achieved. The head custodian should also model the kinds of interaction with adults and students that help establish and maintain a high level of customer service.

First Impressions: Service

When I leave my car to approach any school, I immediately begin looking around for signs of systemic improvements related to customer service. For example, are the visitor parking spaces close to the building or relatively far away? Are they clearly marked? Do there appear to be enough of them? Approaching the front door of the building, and faced with a row of many possible doors, is the one unlocked door clearly marked? (If not, I invariably try that one *last*.) If there is someone at a small table in the front hallway, am I greeted right away? Does the greeter do so with a smile? Does the "visitor process" seem to be clear, and does it appear at first glance to be efficient? Once I enter the front office, am I greeted once again in a timely manner? Does the person doing the greeting stand and approach the counter? Any process-improvement team spotlighting customer service needs to *think like a visitor* and consider what the front-hallway and front office staff does and needs to do when it comes to creating a first impression. Those who are on the front lines in terms of first contact need to be well represented on any improvement team formed to deal with this issue. These questions need to be asked and answered: What constitutes great customer service? How can our customer service processes result in the creation of raving fans on the part of those who have business in our building? If there are barriers to providing first-rate customer service, how can they be removed? How do we at the front door or office deal with our internal customers (teachers, students, support staff)? Would a short, anonymous survey of our internal customers tell us something about what constitutes great customer service for them?

The office manager, in collaboration with the office staff, needs to establish an efficient process to answer phones and provide positive customer service to the public that call or enter the building. The process should include how many times a phone is allowed to ring prior to a voice answering the phone and the number of seconds it should take a staff member to address an individual at the counter. Again, it helps for process-improvement teams to think like the phone caller. Positive customer service is important to building a happy school community, and administrators should make certain that these customer-service issues are evaluated on a regular basis, *not just when something goes wrong.*

Bus Arrival and Departure

These processes are critical, particularly in middle school, because the longer the students sit on a bus that is not moving, the more likely they are to get into mischief. The key is to be able to quickly track which buses have arrived in order to determine if a bus is late or missed a stop. The departure is equally as important. The transportation coordinator needs to know which buses have arrived for dismissal and which are held up in traffic. Buses also have to be organized so that those with routes farthest from the school are grouped together and can be the first set dismissed. The most important thing is to get students home quickly and safely. In Appendix B, we'll take a look at how one elementary school tackled the issue of safety and efficiency with the loading and unloading of buses.

Cafeteria: Lines

Many cafeterias have à la cart and regular, full-lunch lines. The lunch line process needs to be thought out carefully in order to get all students fed in a fast and efficient manner. The best people to ask for input are those who work in the cafeteria to monitor process during lunch bells. They have a keen idea as to how many students are simply buying a drink or a snack and how many are buying a full lunch. Teams can work to improve efficiency, and efficiency is the lifeblood of a well-run school cafeteria. There is also an important customer-service element at work here. I have been in school lunch lines where it was obvious that the cafeteria employees had taken the time to learn the names of students and displayed a wonderful sense of humor; by so doing, those employees made the cafeteria a welcoming place. In one elementary cafeteria, classical music was playing softly in the background.

Cafeteria: Cleanliness

Over the years, I have been in school lunchrooms where there was not a bit of paper or clutter of any sort on the floor, on the tables, or in the lunch lines. On the other hand, I was once in a high school cafeteria where it was difficult to walk through the room without stepping on paper, plastic, or something that was once edible and recently discarded. The difference between these two lunchrooms, I can guarantee, is a systemic approach to improvement. The adults in one building put in place a system composed of measurable processes that ensured the cafeteria was safe and clean. In the other building, the adults simply surrendered to the kids. The contrast here is a good example of how *processes need constant attention*; they need to be evaluated constantly in search of interventions and innovations that will get the job done.

Copy Room

All staff members need copies at one time or another, and administration watches the budget to get the biggest bang for the buck. One of the easiest ways to provide staff with the paper or copies they need while keeping the copy machines in good working condition is to come up with a process for staff to get the copies they need in a timely and efficient manner. Teams might be formed to look at ways to save paper—and trees—during the course of the school year. Also, as teachers find ways to replace the ubiquitous worksheets with other, more engaging activities (that don't require reams of paper), the school and the district save money, *and teachers find ways to get students involved to a greater extent in their own learning*. The results amount to a more learner-centered classroom *and* fewer reams of paper.

Technology

If the school does not have enough equipment for each teacher, the check-out process needs to be quick and easy for teachers. In schools where audio-visual equipment of all kinds may be at a premium, an equitable check-out system needs to be in place to encourage teachers to use the technology as often as possible, giving them equal access to working equipment. Maintenance needs to be a priority and is fair game for a process-improvement team that can give input to those in charge of the equipment, as well as assist in the upkeep of the equipment by providing teachers with a simple checklist of items that will help extend the life and maintain the efficiency of the technology. Just as keeping the building clean should not be the sole responsibility of the custodial staff, the maintenance of critical pieces of expensive instructional technology should be the responsibility of those who use it and those who govern its usage.

Summer School Registration

Summer school registration is a difficult process with a very short turnaround time. It is very frustrating for parents to enroll their children in summer school, so the process needs to be as efficient and friendly as possible. Many school divisions have one or two host sites for summer school. That means that many of the parents are registering students at a school that is not the home school. The registration process needs to be thought out clearly so parents can move quickly from one line to the next and get out as quickly as possible. It may be that a process-improvement team brought together to look at summer school registration should include parents, administrators, and other stakeholders.

Room-Cleaning Process

Schools have a lot of square footage, and it is important to have a clean and tidy building not only for appearance but also for the safety and well-being of students and staff. As part of a continuous-improvement cycle, a team can be formed to find out how custodians and teachers can support each other toward a common goal—a beautiful, safe, and absolutely clean classroom. Teachers are often gone before the night custodians come to work. This means they rarely get to see, much less know, each other. A smart building principal can arrange for everyone to meet and socialize, and that can be followed by a series of meetings intended to streamline whatever processes are in place at night in order to meet the needs of the teachers and students who inhabit the rooms during the day.

New teachers, who are understandably excited and anxious about the coming school year, may well enjoy arranging and decorating their classrooms early. Being able to do this before all teachers report allows them to do whatever needs to be done during that busy week without worrying about room setup. A team composed of the head custodian, an administrator, a teacher mentor, and a second-year teacher who may have a unique perspective on what it was like for her last year can work on rearranging the summer cleaning schedule in order to facilitate new teachers, and that same team (with a new teacher representative each year) can revisit the system in place to get rooms ready during the summer.

Guidance and Student Registration

There is nothing more frustrating to parents than to come and register their children for a new school and be sent away more than once with paperwork and medical documentation that needs to be completed. A clear and precise registration process must be established, and a qualified staff member should be present for potential new registrants to arrive. Part of customer service is to make people feel welcome and wanted in a new school; you want your guidance staff to be warm and welcoming to new students and families as they will remember the first impression they are given by anyone with whom they come into contact during that first visit. Unfortunately, one negative experience while they are in the building will cancel out several positive experiences during that same visit. This may mean that customer-service training needs to be made part of the regular order of business in that building or that district. It is also necessary to evaluate whatever processes are put in place over time, with feedback from parents and other visitors that can inform the improvement process.

Student Early Release and Late Arrival

A safe and secure early-dismissal and late-arrival process for students needs to be established at every school. All schools have a process in place; however, it needs to be evaluated for effectiveness and to decrease the amount of instructional time lost. Once again, a team composed of faculty, parents, front-office personnel, and administrators could be formed for the purpose of evaluating whatever process is in place. Those stakeholders each bring a different perspective to the table, and their diverse viewpoints can contribute to a strong, effective process that does not result in long waits in the office on the part of students, with the attendant lost instructional time that entails.

Ordering Custodial and Office Supplies

Nothing is more frustrating for teachers and support personnel than to run out of supplies at a critical time. When this happens, people are quick to play the blame game and slow to look for root causes. The fact is that running out of something may be the result of inefficient or broken processes. Blaming people is, after all, easier than taking the time to visit and evaluate whatever processes are in place at the moment. If the status quo when it comes to ordering supplies and materials is not acceptable, then the status quo needs changing. Administrators can, once again, put together a process-improvement team that can spend the time necessary to determine what is not working and fix it. Don't blame people, fix the process.

Safety and Hall Travel

Most schools have some type of fire drill or evacuation drill procedure as required by law. The process truly needs to be studied with decisions made to get students and staff out of the building quickly and safely, as well as to be able to account for all students and staff. In every school, administrators can bring together a team to study the flow of traffic in the halls and reduce the amount of congestion and time spent during hall travel in order to increase the amount of instructional time in all classes. Noisy hallways take away from the effectiveness of teachers and students who have created a positive and smooth-running classroom environment only to be adversely affected by what is going on in the halls. Once again, it is easy to blame people (students for being too noisy, teachers for not supervising students); it is more difficult—but more effective—to search for solutions among broken processes crying out for improvement or replacement.

Custodial Process for
Opening and Closing a Building

In an age when safety and saving money are at the top of anyone's to-do list when it comes to building operations, schools can form teams that can serve safety and cost savings but still allow teachers access to their classrooms at certain times outside the normal school day. A process-improvement team might begin with the end in mind: What should the building consistently look like when the doors are unlocked every morning? Working back from that given, a whole series of processes can be put in place that will allow the night staff to arrive at that same destination every morning. A process also needs to be established to systematically close down the building and lock and secure all doors and hallways as well as turn off lights. This would reduce the amount of visits night security needs to make to a building because doors were left open or unlocked. An effective internal evaluation process (quality control on the production line) will reduce the need for external evaluation processes (districtwide quality control) and will result in more consistency.

Restocking of Soap, Paper Towels, and Sanitizer in the Restrooms or Hallways

There are times when I am presenting in a school building when it is apparent that there is no process in place to accommodate adult visitors after hours as it pertains to restrooms. A system that responds only to the needs of the moment is not efficient; repeated problems with restrooms (lack of paper towels, sinks that don't work, faucets that leak or drip constantly, cleanliness issues, graffiti, empty sanitizer dispensers, broken doors) are fixable if a continuous-improvement system is firmly in place. This may mean that once a specific process-improvement team has identified problems and come up with solutions, and the custodial and maintenance staff have followed through with the changes, there needs to be a way of soliciting feedback from anyone who uses the restrooms (students, teachers, parents, visitors—everyone) so that adjustments can be made when necessary. In the case of after-hours use of the facilities, a schedule of activities needs to be established and updated, and day and night custodians need to coordinate who does what and when, with excellent customer service as the end game.

Graffiti

I have been in schools where graffiti stays on the restroom walls, apparently for lack of an efficient set of processes that might result in clean restrooms all the time. I have also been in restrooms that would make any four-star restaurant proud. One had beautiful, live plants . . . and this was a *student* restroom. Teams of students were in charge of helping the custodial staff keep them clean. Teams, possibly composed of custodians, students, and faculty, can establish a process to inspect the outside building as well as bathroom stalls, hall walls, and lockers for graffiti. Graffiti needs to be removed immediately so students see a well-kept building when they enter in the morning and have no need to gossip about any graffiti because there won't be any if the custodial team identifies and removes graffiti prior to student arrival. Building interiors should also be monitored throughout the day to eliminate or deter any graffiti that may occur during the school day. Once again, it is a matter of process: Processes for dealing with graffiti can be brainstormed, arrived at, put in place, and evaluated on a regular basis. This also includes a workable and enforced process to deal with those who deface school property.

Floors

The custodial team spends hours cleaning floors as well as stripping and waxing floors. The team needs to study the most-traveled hallways and identify floors that need to be maintained throughout the year with wax and polish, and determine which areas can be put on a rotating system so it doesn't take the custodial staff an entire break to clean floors. If floors are maintained throughout the school year, the custodial team can maintain a certain look instead of only having it at the beginning of the school year and after holiday breaks. The idea here is to start not with how things have been done but with how the floors should look most of the time. The condition of floors throughout the building says a good deal about the quest for quality on the part of all stakeholders, not just on the part of the custodial team. I was in an elementary school where all the chairs in all the classrooms had split tennis balls forced onto the bottoms of the chair legs. This undoubtedly assisted the custodial staff in keeping the floors looking great. It is also a good lesson for the students, especially if they are involved to a large extent in keeping the classrooms clean.

From customer service at the front door to the condition of restrooms and floors throughout the building, everything ought to be subject to the collaborative reflections of process-improvement teams dedicated to quality. This is by no means an exhaustive list of building-related processes, but everything on these pages should be part of the overall continuous-improvement efforts of stakeholders closest to those processes.

In Appendix B, we'll look at what one elementary school did to improve safety and efficiency in the bus loop.

Appendix B

Building-Level Improvement Example

In a systems-oriented environment, where no process is left unattended or unexamined, improvements are legion at the building or classroom level. This includes, as we saw in Appendix A, the bus loop. When it comes to unloading students in the morning and picking them up again in the afternoon, principals are single-minded. One principal I know ends his Friday-before-the-kids-arrive-for-the-first-day-of-school meeting with, "And finally, the most important thing is that the students all arrive home safely on Monday!" Students arrive for the new school year after a long summer break, and the bus numbers and drivers may be totally different from last year; those first few days can be nerve-wracking for students, staff, and parents alike. It is to everyone's advantage that the bus-loop processes be combined into a workable system, complete with a regular evaluation of its effectiveness.

At Pembroke Elementary, a Virginia school with a high special-education population, the administrative team was not satisfied with the way the system worked for either the morning arrival or the afternoon departure of the buses. In this large school district, buses arrive from all over the city, and their arrival times vary greatly, according to Assistant Principal Karen O'Meara. As a new assistant principal, O'Meara noticed much confusion in the bus loop, particularly at the *end* of the school day. Students, teachers, and teacher assistants were often confused as to where their students' buses were parked, and it became apparent to O'Meara that something had to be done; more than that, a system for unloading and loading students had to be put in place that would result in safety, efficiency, and *consistency*. Principal Linda Hayes empowered O'Meara and

Grant Baker, the school's administrative assistant, to work with staff to identify problems and find solutions. The number of special-needs students, those who needed wheelchairs and someone to accompany them to the bus loop, underscored the need for a smooth-functioning system that would stand the test of time and the analysis of the team formed to change or adjust the various key processes involved.

The timely loan of some bright yellow AAA safety vests helped O'Meara, Baker, and two teacher assistants bring order to the offloading of students in the morning. "The real test," according to O'Meara, "was coming up with a plan for the afternoon dismissal" (personal correspondence, September 16, 2010). Using a diagram that divided the arriving buses into inner and outer loops, a bus monitor with a walkie-talkie stood at the outer entrance to the loops, announcing the arrival of a particular bus to a *second* monitor, "who would verify the slot number, bus number, and record it on the laminated poster with a dry erase marker. This allowed the teachers and teacher assistants to locate each student's bus immediately and begin loading the student," says O'Meara. Once all buses were loaded, the signal was given for the first bus on the outer loop to proceed, with all buses in that loop following. After the last outer-loop bus pulled out, the inner-loop buses followed suit.

Now—and this is an important part of this whole continuous-improvement effort—O'Meara and Baker timed the whole departure process, from the first bus to the last, and their baseline was fifteen minutes. As teachers, teacher assistants, bus drivers, and students became more familiar with the process, the time decreased until they were able to get everyone out of the loop in nine minutes. According to O'Meara, the bus drivers were particularly happy, because each of them had another bus route to complete following the elementary bus-route run.

This new bus-loop system for loading and unloading students was beneficial in many ways:

1. The smooth operation that resulted from this team's continuous-improvement process led to increased safety for students and everyone else involved.

2. Buses were now inserted into the appropriate loop in an orderly fashion.

3. Intentional bus placement allowed for better access for lifting ramps for wheelchair-bound students.

4. Teachers and teacher assistants were better able to locate the right bus with the use of the laminated board showing the positioning of each bus.

5. The time needed to load and depart decreased by almost half.

O'Meara and her team continue to evaluate their bus-loop system, and they have recently added a process whereby bus drivers, on the first day of school, place a colored dot on the clothing of students as they exit the bus in the morning. Classroom teachers have a color-coded bus chart, with the bus numbers and the corresponding color code. The teacher records the bus number, and at the end of the day, each bus has a number *and* a color in the window as the students approach the buses. Cut-out, colored, and numbered buses are placed on the direction chart using Velcro strips. The students check the board and walk directly to their buses. All this improves efficiency for students and teachers alike.

The bus-loop system at Pembroke Elementary is composed of many individual processes that work together to increase efficiency and safety. Furthermore, it is crystal clear that *without considerable reflection*, along with a willingness to take some risks, this creation of an effective system for loading and unloading students would not have happened. Principal Linda Hayes empowered the improvement team to do what was necessary, and the results, as we have seen, benefitted everyone involved. This is a great example of what can be done when processes are put under the microscope by a team willing to question and seriously analyze the status quo—all in the name of continuous improvement.

Appendix C

Processes Into Systems: Classroom Level

While building-level improvements support instruction, sometimes in a rather oblique fashion, classroom-level systems are composed of processes that directly affect teacher performance and academic growth. I once observed a classroom where one student after another went to the restroom in what seemed to be like a relay race. The hall pass got handed off to the next student, who in turn looked for the next taker when coming back into the classroom. The stated process for leaving the classroom to go to the restroom may have been different, but in this case the process had been hijacked by students who were, one after another, missing out on whatever learning was on offer in that room. Processes, taken together, constitute systems; in this case, the entire classroom-management system had broken down over time, as each separate process (leaving the classroom, sharpening a pencil, getting ready for the next activity) went unpracticed and ultimately untended.

The classroom system as it relates to assessment is composed of smaller processes (the administering of quizzes and tests, the timely return of said quizzes and tests, the giving of feedback, the number of formative assessments) that contribute to the academic growth of students. Good processes that run smoothly help students become better at what they do and contribute to what they understand; an effective system of assessment is only as good as its component parts. If the process for giving feedback is weak, it weakens the overall effectiveness of the system. Teachers who do not use an item analysis (process) to find their own weak areas of instruction weaken the delivery system they have in place. Teachers who ignore the fact that classroom movement (process) positively affects learning and memory will pay a price for keeping students seated for long periods of time. Once again, the system breaks down because the individual processes that compose it go unused or untended over time.

The following are some typical classroom-specific processes that need to be evaluated by teachers in order to determine what improvements need to be made, if any, in order to make them ever more effective. As with the building-level list, this is not meant to be definitive or complete; it will, I trust, provide a starting place for teachers who are willing to look at how they do what they do in the name of continuous improvement.

Movement

In *Brain Rules: 12 Principles for Surviving and Thriving at Work, Home, and School,* John Medina (2008) points out that "our evolutionary ancestors were used to walking up to 12 miles *per day*" (p. 23). Our brains developed during that time, and exercise was an important part of that development. Medina goes on to say, "We were not used to sitting in classrooms for 8 hours at a stretch" (p. 24). Movement sends blood to our brains, and that blood contains oxygen and glucose, both critical to the learning process. Yet I observe classrooms where students are required to sit for long periods of time because conventional wisdom tells us that students can concentrate better that way. Actually, students are better able to concentrate when they have had the benefit of physical exercise through physical education classes, through recess, and as a result of classroom processes that purposefully harness movement as a learning tool.

Teachers should look at their lesson plans and incorporate movement (charting in groups, standing to meet with a partner, going to the side of the room to secure handouts, taking a brain break by doing some simple exercises lasting only a couple of minutes, or just plain standing and stretching every so often) into those plans every few minutes. For example, rather than have students share with a partner something while seated, have them stand and move to find a partner with whom they can discuss what they just observed in a short video, or heard in a short lecture. Add a bit of upbeat music to the process and students get the break they need, along with the conversation that helps them process information—all in a very structured and intentional way.

Student-to-Student Conversations

Students remember and understand more when they are given the opportunity to share information with each other in a structured way. Teachers can experiment with students talking in pairs, trios, or quartets. It is advisable that before students do this, they discuss with the teacher what it takes to be a good listener. Students at almost any age know what can derail a conversation, and by extension, they know basically what is required if two students want to have a successful and substantive conversation (eye contact, supportive body language and facial expressions, the ability to ask for summaries or ask for points of clarification). The teacher can draw this out of them, charting their input in a way that provides a baseline for good communication whether they are in pairs or larger groups.

More than just charting and posting the chart permanently on the wall is needed, however, if the whole classroom's communication system is to work properly. The process has to be evaluated frequently by the students. I know teachers who use a listening-skills chart to conduct postconversation discussions about how successful the students were in their last paired or group discussion. The initial brainstorming and the posting of the chart is useless unless the process includes constant evaluation in the name of continuous improvement. In this case, the students do something (a paired discussion, for example), evaluate it (using the chart as a reference point), and then make adjustments as needed the next time around. The teacher's job is to facilitate all this in a way that leads to progress over time; otherwise, these student-to-student interactions will most certainly break down, at which point the teacher may simply stop using a great process simply because the evaluation tool was in place (or used) to gauge its effectiveness and then *improve* that process.

Transitions and Directions

The enemy of any classroom process is confusion. I have observed classrooms where a transition between activities that should have taken a minute or so takes much too long. I have seen teachers give *several* auditory directions in quick succession, only to have to walk around the room in an attempt to give bits and pieces of that same set of instructions over and over again to various students who did not listen or understand what was said the first time around. Giving clear, precise directions one at a time will save time and allow the teacher to observe that, for example, each student has a book, a pencil, a writing journal, and a handout, and that the book is opened to a certain page. If a picture is indeed worth a thousand words (of directions), teachers can project on the screen a picture of exactly what the desk should look like, removing any time-wasting ambiguity or downright chaos. Teachers who are willing to take a close, objective look at transition periods and the whole process involved in giving directions should be able to improve those processes to the point where there is no wasted time or confusion.

Formative Assessment

Summative assessments normally come at the end of a chapter, unit, semester, or school year; grades are given, and everyone moves on. Formative assessments are used to provide various forms of feedback along the way to a finished product. Students working on an essay, for example, receive constant feedback (from teachers, peer review, checklists and rubrics) on draft after draft, making corrections and adjustments until it is complete. Examples of formative assessments would be informal teacher questions and conversations with students as teachers check for understanding. Other examples would be student portfolios, reflective journals, and presentation rehearsals (Burke, 2010). All these serve as benchmarks and accelerants for students on the continuous-improvement highway. Each of these processes is a component of the system of overall assessment that teachers need to be experimenting with and evaluating over time, *and feedback is an indispensable component of each of these processes.*

Feedback

The quality and quantity of feedback given to students is critical, and teachers need to take a look at their feedback process. When I first started teaching, I used to put checkmarks on homework papers to indicate it was "acceptable" (whatever that meant), or I would often add a hearty "Well done!" (whatever that meant) on a few papers that I considered outstanding. Of course, neither of these comments was effective as feedback for students trying to improve their skills or increase their knowledge. As September turned into October, the amount of homework assignments I got back steadily decreased, and I blamed the students, the parents, the textbook, and the weather, while all the time I was clueless about what kinds of feedback might have actually helped my students improve on whatever it was I wanted them to be doing.

As we saw earlier in the book, feedback must be timely, specific, and corrective in nature. It must provide students with information that informs their individual continuous-improvement journeys. Feedback as a process supports the entire assessment system that, in turn, supports student progress. Students really have to know what they can do to improve, and feedback (provided on papers that are returned, given through individual conferences) must inform them or remind them of exactly what needs to be done to improve performance.

Teacher feedback, important as it is, can be supplemented by the feedback provided by checklists and rubrics. These devices allow students to check their own work in real time and make quantitative adjustments based on a checklist (Does the paragraph have a topic sentence?) or qualitative changes based on a rubric (Is the paper well organized, supporting the writer's position throughout?). Burke (2010) affirms that "feedback is the heart and soul of formative assessment" (p. 21). Formative assessment, as Burke defines it, is labeled such "when the purpose for using it is to provide constructive and specific feedback early in the learning process" (p. 144). Teachers who have their students work their way through several drafts of an essay over time—with plenty of corrective feedback in the form of checklists, rubrics, and teacher-provided written and oral feedback—contribute in large measure to their students' ability to write effectively.

Processes Used at the Beginning and the End of Class

There are two times during classes where time is, as they say, "a wastin'" in a big way: the first five minutes and the last five minutes. The most effective classrooms I have seen are those in which students know exactly what to do when they come into the room, and whatever it is that they do is accomplished while the teacher *greets students* as they enter. The what-to-do-when-entering-the-room process is so embedded in the overall management system in these classrooms that much is accomplished up front, and with little fuss and not much bother.

I was once observing in an elementary classroom at the beginning of a day that had been marked by a two-hour snow delay. In spite of everything—the weather, late buses, lots of snow gear—those third graders entered the room and, to the accompaniment of an upbeat song, put their gear away, gathered their materials, and were ready to go within short order. What to do when entering the room was so ingrained that there was little confusion, and the teacher was able to greet them, unencumbered by having to remind anyone of anything. The process had become routine, and although there was a bit more delay due to late buses and dealing with all that cold-weather clothing, it was a smooth transition.

I have also observed classrooms where the first five minutes and the last five minutes (ten minutes of valuable time) are wasted as processes that may have been established early in the school year have fallen by the wayside. Multiply that ten minutes by 180 days, and real time is being squandered, all because the teacher does not regularly evaluate critical processes that make up the classroom-management system. Effective teachers don't need a chart on the wall to tell students what the procedures are; they have practiced it so many times it has become truly routine. A welcome side effect of any deeply rooted and front-loaded management process is that a teacher does not have to continually remind Johnny, Eddie, Mary, and Maurice of anything— *they know what to do and they do it.* If the teacher sees signs that the process is unraveling, she will revisit it with her students in order to get whatever it is back on track and running smoothly.

Technology as a Tool, Not an End

During my days as an elementary and secondary student, I can remember blackboards that covered as many as three out of four walls in the classroom, and it was possible in many classes for every student to find a place at the board, where we worked our way through math problems or diagrammed sentences. Going to the board had the added benefit of giving us a chance to stand and move in the classroom. Blackboards amounted to pretty basic stuff as technology goes, but it is what we had, and many of our teachers put it to good use.

As a Baby Boomer and digital immigrant, I am often bedazzled by what I see on smart boards and other interactive screens; I still find it amazing that someone can place a finger on a screen and manipulate or move a graphic or a piece of text. Digital natives, on the other hand, grew up with the technology and can do the same on a hand-held device with which they are perfectly familiar and which holds no mysteries for them.

There is danger here for teachers just beginning to become familiar with the wonders of this technology. I have been in classrooms where a teacher will bring a student up front in order to manipulate something on the screen. While the teacher works with one or more students up front, their classmates are verbally invited to participate in their minds, anticipating or predicting what the student coming to the screen should do in order to correctly solve the problem or complete the activity. As I watch students from the side of the room, however, I can say with virtual certainty that many of them have gone to a better place in their minds. Also, once the student who is currently at the board sits down, he can now go to that better place in *his* mind, safe in the knowledge that his turn at the front of the room (and in the line of fire) is over. Another danger here is that some students are embarrassed to be the only one at the board, and this may serve to inhibit performance on the part of a student who is normally able to solve the problem or complete the activity at his desk.

If every student in the room cannot be directly involved in what is happening on the screen at the front of the room, teachers need to put in place a process that involves them in some way from their seats. It may be—and I have seen this used effectively—that seated students have small white boards and markers that allow them, in pairs or individually, to become engaged simultaneously. If a second adult is available, she can monitor the seat-based activities while the teacher works with individuals, pairs, or groups at the front of the room. It is also possible that students could stand and discuss in pairs or trios what they think ought to be done, after which they can be invited to share their conclusions. For example, a paragraph in need of serious grammatical help could be posted on the screen, and students working in standing trios or quartets could be put to work trying to find and fix the mistakes. Ways need to be found to involve every student in the room at any given time; it is not realistic to think that what is happening with two or three students at the front of the room is going to enthrall their classmates or otherwise mentally engage them in the activity.

As cell phones find their ways into the hands of every student, many teachers are creatively using the technology in a way that allows students to text information onto the screen as part of a brainstorming session. Students who have just read an essay could "vote" with their cell phones, deciding whether what they just read was a persuasive or informational essay. As the voting continues, the results appear on the screen in bar-graph form; once the voting is done, the teacher can seek input from students as to why they voted the way they did. In both of these examples, cell phones are enlisted as convenient tools as the means to an end. As each year passes, more and more teachers are incorporating such tools into their practice, but care needs to be taken to ensure that the processes are smooth and efficient.

Teacher Talk as a Process

When I first started teaching, I thought talking was teaching. My subject area in those days was U.S. history, and I was a master at using the overhead projector. I uncovered those priceless transparency notes one by one and lectured for large chunks of time. My students took notes, and the idea was that they would go home, "study" the notes (whatever that meant), and perform well on my summative tests and quizzes. I would grade said tests and quizzes, record the grades, and move on to the next chapter and the next chronological period of American history.

The irony of all this teacher talk I unleashed on my students was that I was the one who learned the most during the course of every year. Why? Because I talked the most. My lecture–take notes–study–take quizzes or tests system was composed of several processes, of course: the way I presented the material, the way my students took notes, the way we reviewed subject material, and the way they "studied" for tests at home. The system was broken, for several reasons:

- Trying to concentrate on what I was saying and take notes at the same time, my students must have been particularly frustrated, because I provided no time at all for students to process material in the classroom. Any processing was to be done at home, long after the notes had been taken. My fantasy was always that they took a little time each evening to go over the notes and process parallel material in the textbook. I did say fantasy, right?
- When I conducted my review sessions in class, I concentrated on terms, dates, vocabulary, events, and the names of politicians, generals, inventors—all the information that lived at the bottom level of the cognitive ladder (knowledge). In fact, I was the only one who lived at the second level of the cognitive ladder (comprehension) during the course of the school year.

I explained, elucidated, illustrated, pontificated, described, and summarized, and by so doing, I was the one who developed a fairly deep understanding of U.S. history.

During my early years of teaching, it never occurred to me to subject my processes to any sort of analysis or evaluation in an attempt to improve what I did. It was easy to blame other factors for my students' poor test performance: the textbook reading level, too many years of history to cover in one year, the parents, uncomfortable desks, bad lighting, inconsistent room temperature, and—most unfortunate of all—the fact that "kids today (early 1970s) just don't want to learn" in the way that *we* did when *we* were young.

There is nothing wrong with lecture, provided students have an opportunity to process the material in class, with each other, and immediately after new information has been presented. The same is true of videos, which should be mercifully short and should be followed by periods of student-to-student processing and reflection. This allows students to take what they already know about a subject, work in the new information, and arrive at a new level of understanding. A teacher's delivery system is composed of many processes, and each of those processes should be open to scrutiny, held up to the light, and put under the microscope in an attempt to gauge its effectiveness as a teaching and learning tool.

Those who do the talking do the learning, as I found out in my first several years of teaching. I rarely, if ever, had my students share information with each other. They did not turn to a partner and talk, stand and share in a trio, or learn what makes a good listener—along with why listening is such an important part of communication. I stood, while they sat. I talked, while they listened or went to a better place in their minds. I moved, while they hunkered down in their seats and thought of novel reasons to go somewhere—anywhere—to avoid sitting for long periods of time. It never once occurred to me that what I had created was a broken system, composed of dysfunctional processes, and that the lack of quality apparent to me in my reflective moments was something I could have changed had I been willing to analyze my instructional system for fundamental weaknesses and strengths, making changes in an attempt to make what I did on a daily basis better. Teachers and administrators must not be afraid to look at *how* they do *what* they do at every turn, and while this is not always comfortable, it is necessary if processes and systems are to be improved. This continuous-improvement process can be accomplished by individual teachers or by teams of teachers working in tandem in order to move down the continuous-improvement highway.

In Appendix D, we'll look at the success stories of three teachers working respectively with students in the second, fourth, and sixth grades.

Appendix D

Classroom-Level Improvement Examples

W hile great gains can be made in the area of customer service and building-level improvements of all kinds, it is critical that teachers, buildings, and districts concentrate heavily on classroom-level process and system improvements. While face-to-face training sessions and online courses can certainly contribute to continuous improvement, this will only happen if teachers examine *how* they do *what* they do in their classrooms, followed by a commitment to make necessary and meaningful adjustments in key processes related to management and instruction. This can happen when teachers work in teams or individually. The real power of improvement lies in a willingness to look at everything with an eye toward how it can be improved.

School districts can accelerate improvement by seriously and consistently backing improvement efforts in classrooms at all levels. The Fort Bend Independent School District, in Sugar Land, Texas, is, as of this writing, in its third straight school year of providing resources and incentives to teachers willing to conduct their own action research projects in the name of continuous improvement. Yuping Anselm, Fort Bend's coordinator of research and program evaluation, spearheaded this effort at finding teacher researchers willing to fully participate in a program dedicated to conducting action research at the classroom level.

In many districts, credit for professional development is awarded to those who complete face-to-face training sessions or online courses. In the second year of its efforts related to continuous improvement, Fort Bend made the decision to provide the full total of fourteen required credits to teachers who successfully took part in the action research program. "Since we deem action research is an alternative form of professional development," says Anselm, "it makes sense to award professional-development credits to [teachers] for their efforts" (personal communication, September 8, 2010). The district, realizing the time commitment made by teachers in the writing of their research papers, also provides a monetary stipend to teachers who complete the project.

The Fort Bend program has produced some interesting and significant results, as individual teachers and teacher teams improve their own performance, and that of their students, as a direct result of the action research projects. One such successful effort at continuous improvement came when fourth-grade teacher Sarah Erschabek instituted an entirely optional book club for her students *on Saturdays.* There were no grades or assignments, yet thirty-six of forty-one students agreed to give up time on weekends to take part in this attempt to jump-start or accelerate a love of reading for fun on the part of Erschabek's fourth graders. The book club did not meet at school; indeed, they met one Saturday each month at the house of a different student. Erschabek reports that support among parents was high, and one parent said, "I cannot believe how much my daughter has changed over this school year. I think this book club is a wonderful idea, and my daughter is reading more than she's ever read before" (personal communication, September 6, 2010). Anecdotal evidence to be sure, but powerful nevertheless.

In addition to data showing that the number of Erschabek's students who preferred English language arts (including reading and writing) to other subjects jumped from 29 percent in the fall to 44 percent in the spring (more than any other single subject), their reading levels also increased, as measured by DRA2 scores and other comparative data. Significantly, at the conclusion of the seven Saturdays, 78 percent of the book club members surveyed said that reading was an interesting or great way to spend time, while that figure was just 39 percent for non–club members. Book club members also improved their writing scores over the course of the year to a greater extent than nonmembers.

One of the amazing things about the results of these Saturday book club sessions is that *all this was accomplished without assigning grades.* Erschabek's fourth graders willingly read the books, discussed with each other what they read, and derived pleasure from doing so—all to their immediate and long-term benefit. During the course of the year, students recommended books to Erschabek and to each other, in person and via blogs set up by Erschabek, to which she and club members had access. According to Erschabek, the blogs for this new school year will remain open to those who participated last year, giving them a constant source of intellectual stimulation as they are able to see and comment on what is being read and discussed by a new group of book club members. At this writing, Erschabek is making adjustments to the program, based on her own observations, as well as feedback received from book club participants. She will move forward with what she has found to be an enjoyable and ultimately rewarding accelerator for student and teacher growth.

Finally, and importantly, Erschabek's growing confidence in her own ability to harness the power of action research in the cause of continuous improvement will serve her and her fourth graders well in the coming years. The whole idea of examining processes, making necessary adjustments, and regularly doing it all over again is the essence of continuous improvement.

Moving from the fourth to the sixth grade, middle school ELA teacher Hallie Antweil has also experienced a great deal of success with taking the time to hook her students on books, getting them to read on their own and for pleasure. Antweil increased her chances of success by offering a wide choice of books for her students, choosing books that she "knew would appeal to a wide range of readers, even reluctant ones" (personal communication, September 6, 2010). Antweil chose books she had read and spent class time showing her sixth graders the books, letting them handle them, and intriguing them by talking briefly about the plot of each book. In this age of technologically savvy students, Antweil took every opportunity to tie in the books with a website's book trailer, if it existed, and she made certain that some of the books on offer were technology based. In addition, some *books* actually had their own websites, and students were able to visit these sites in order to discover whether or not they were interested in checking out or purchasing the book.

As of this writing, Antweil has introduced what she calls "personal book talks" into the mix. Her sixth graders go to the library every two weeks, and, knowing which students may not be disposed to check out a book on their own, she will "make a bee-line for these students, and I interview them individually to find out what types of books they might be interested in" (personal communication, September 6, 2010). Based on what she already knows about the student, along with what she has gleaned from the interview, Antweil will take him to the shelf and to a book she thinks he is most likely to read. She then tells him a bit about the plot, explaining why *she* really enjoyed the book. At this point, says Antweil, the student "is pretty psyched to check out the book" (personal communication, September 6, 2010).

Each student keeps a reading log that is turned in every two weeks: this gives Antweil an opportunity to have another personal conversation with each student about what he read and what he liked or did not like about the book; it also gives her a chance to recommend books in the same genre or about the same subject. During one of those conversations, Antweil discovered that one student who said she did not really consider herself a reader said she liked fictional books with World War II as the subject. Antweil recommended a particular book and was thrilled when the student came back from the library with *two* books by the same author. That student has returned to Antweil for more recommendations and appears to be on the road to reading for pleasure.

Antweil has evaluated her book-talk program and has made some adjustments. Students now make book talks to the entire class, describing their experiences with a book and making recommendations to classmates. Antweil has observed students writing down those recommendations and then following that up by taking out those books from the library. She is now experimenting with having three or four students read the same book and then discuss it together during SSR (sustained silent-reading time), thus introducing the concept of a book club into the process. The next step for Antweil is to set up a wiki or blog so that the discussions and recommendations can move outside the classroom to the blogosphere.

For these two teachers, Sarah Erschabek and Hallie Antweil, there is a constant desire to improve process. Both teachers use student surveys that give them much information about which students think of themselves as readers, which value reading, and which believe they are self-motivated readers. In both cases, reading scores have improved, and the number of those students who read for pleasure has increased—no small thing.

Another Fort Bend teacher who understands the impact of constantly reassessing how he does what he does is Jeff Carrus, a second-grade teacher. Understanding the importance of vocabulary in speaking, writing, and reading, Carrus has, over the years, continued to assess how he deals with it in his classroom. After noticing how his students struggled with vocabulary, Carrus began to incorporate various ways to improve their facility with and comprehension of vocabulary words within the context of his reading program. Over the years, he kept what worked and discarded what did not; most importantly, he never stopped taking risks on behalf of his students, and the way he currently deals with vocabulary has resulted in a high level of success for his second graders.

Every couple of weeks, Carrus chooses four words from the reading his students are doing, as well as two words that may not be included in the reading but for which the text provides various clues. This puts the minds of his students to work as they learn to infer from those clues what the two otherwise unfamiliar words might mean. Carrus also posts the words on a chart; students track the usage of those words as they speak and write about whatever it is they are reading during the next several days. They also practice saying the words until they become familiar with pronunciation, and then he takes all this to the next level.

As he introduces the vocabulary words to his second graders, Carrus provides additional context by giving them examples and nonexamples of usage that would apply to the classroom and to his own personal life. Then, students use a visualization technique that makes understanding the word really personal (Figure D.1). They also work with synonyms and antonyms during that two-week period, and at the end of the unit Carrus and his students "celebrate the word that we used most frequently by acting it out as a class" (personal communication, September 2010).

Anyone interested in continuous improvement is constantly checking for results, and Carrus has results that provide ample evidence that what he is doing is working. Since he put this system in place, "student scores have soared in vocabulary, and they use these words all the time. The vocabulary test grades have been steadily above 90," Carrus reports, and students "are using the new words anywhere from 70–100 times per unit." Most important, perhaps, according to Carrus, "Students now look forward to vocabulary because it is fun, and they get to share their own visualizations and experiences with the words" (personal communication, September 2010). On top of this, Carrus has received the constant support of his students' parents, who are

Figure D.1 One of Jeff Carrus's students created this visualization of the vocabulary word "destination." Such visualization helps Carrus's second graders with comprehension.

amazed at how their second graders are improving their own writing, speaking, and reading skills.

Not only do students enjoy working with vocabulary as part of their reading units; their vocabulary scores highlight the success Carrus is having by having them personalize usage with visualization and personal examples. Figure D.2 shows the pre- and posttest vocabulary scores through four units. In addition, his students' DRA scores increased dramatically since he began using this new methodology for teaching vocabulary. As of this writing, Carrus is well into another school year with this system, and he will continue to evaluate its effectiveness over time, all to the benefit of his second graders at Barrington Place Elementary.

Figure D.2   Mean Pre- and Posttest Scores

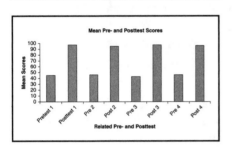

These three outstanding Fort Bend teachers, Sarah Erschabek, Hallie Antweil, and Jeff Carrus, all understand that improvement is not a one-shot deal; it is an ongoing journey. One group of students replaces another, and each year brings adjustments and improvements to processes and systems that, while effective, can always be made more so by teachers who are never fully at rest, never satisfied with the status quo, and ever in search of something that works better that what they are currently using. These master teachers are lifelong learners willing to take risks on behalf of kids in a never-ending journey down the continuous-improvement highway.

References

Blase, J., Blase, J., & Phillips, D. (2010). *Handbook of school improvement: How high-performing principals create high-performing schools*. Thousand Oaks, CA: Corwin.

Bluestein, J. (2008). *The win-win classroom: A fresh and positive look at classroom management*. Thousand Oaks, CA: Corwin.

Bluestein, J. (2010). *Becoming a win-win teacher: Survival strategies for the beginning educator*. Thousand Oaks, CA: Corwin.

Brooks, J., & Brooks, M. (1999). *In search of understanding: The case for constructivist classrooms*. Alexandria, VA: Association for Supervision and Curriculum Development.

Brown, T. (2009). *Change by design: How design thinking transforms organizations and inspires innovation*. New York: HarperCollins.

Burke, K. (2006). *From standards to rubrics in 6 steps* (Rev. ed.). Thousand Oaks, CA: Corwin.

Burke, K. (2008). *What to do with the kid who . . .: Developing cooperation, self-discipline, and responsibility in the classroom* (3rd ed.). Thousand Oaks, CA: Corwin.

Burke, K. (2010). *Balanced assessment: From formative to summative*. Bloomington, IN: Solution Tree.

Collins, J. (2001). *Good to great: Why some companies make the leap . . . and others don't*. New York: HarperCollins.

Conzemius, A., & O'Neill, J. (2002). *The handbook for SMART school teams*. Bloomington, IN: National Educational Service.

Conzemius, A., & O'Neill, J. (2006). *The power of SMART goals: Using goals to improve student learning*. Bloomington, IN: Solution Tree.

Costa, A. (2008). *The school as a home for the mind: Creating mindful curriculum, instruction, and dialogue*. Thousand Oaks, CA: Corwin.

Covington, M. (1992). *Making the grade: A self-worth perspective on motivation and school reform*. New York: Cambridge University Press.

Darling-Hammond, L. (1997). *The right to learn: A blueprint for creating schools that work*. San Francisco: Jossey-Bass.

Darling-Hammond, L. (Ed.). (2008). *Powerful learning: What we know about teaching for understanding*. San Francisco: Jossey-Bass.

Davidovich, R., Nikolay, P., Laugerman, B., & Commodore, C. (2010). *Beyond school improvement: The journey to innovative leadership*. Thousand Oaks, CA: Corwin.

Deci, E. (1995). *Why we do what we do: Understanding self-motivation*. New York: Penguin.

Deming, W. E. (2000). *Out of the crisis*. Cambridge: MIT Press.

Eaker, R., DuFour, R., & DuFour, R. (2002). *Getting started: Reculturing schools to become professional learning communities*. Bloomington, IN: National Educational Service.

Fullan, M. (2010). *Motion leadership: The skinny on becoming change savvy*. Thousand Oaks, CA: Corwin.

Garmston, R., & Wellman, B. (1999). *The adaptive school: A sourcebook for developing collaborative groups*. Norwood, MA: Christopher-Gordon.

Goodlad, J. (2004). *A place called school* (20th anniversary ed.). New York: McGraw-Hill.

Gordon, G. (2006). *Building engaged schools: Getting the most out of America's classrooms.* New York: Gallup.

Hargreaves, A., Earl, L., Moore, S., & Manning, S. (2001). *Learning to change.* San Francisco: Jossey-Bass.

Hord, S., & Sommers, W. (2008). *Leading professional learning communities: Voices from research and practice.* Thousand Oaks, CA: Corwin.

Jenkins, L. (2003). *Improving student learning: Applying Deming's quality principles in the classroom* (2nd ed.). Milwaukee, WI: ASQ.

Jenkins, L. (2005). *Permission to forget: And nine other root causes of America's frustration with education.* Milwaukee, WI: ASQ.

Jensen, E. (2005). *Top tunes for teaching: 977 song titles and practical tools for choosing the right music every time.* San Diego, CA: The Brain Store.

Jones, F. (2007). *Tools for teaching: Discipline, instruction, motivation.* Santa Cruz, CA: Fredric H. Jones & Associates, Inc.

Keene, E. O., & Zimmermann, S. (2007). *Mosaic of thought: The power of comprehension strategy instruction* (2nd ed.). Portsmouth, NH: Heinemann.

Lipton, L., & Wellman, B. (2000). *Pathways to understanding: Patterns and practices in the learning-focused classroom.* Guilford, VT: Pathways Publishing.

Lipton, L., & Wellman, B. (2001). *Mentoring matters: A practical guide to learning-focused relationships.* Sherman, CT: Mira Via.

Marzano, R. (2003a). *Classroom management that works: Research-based strategies for every teacher.* Alexandria, VA: Association for Supervision and Curriculum Development.

Marzano, R. (2003b). *What works in schools: Translating research into action.* Alexandria, VA: Association for Supervision and Curriculum Development.

Marzano, R., Pickering, D., & Pollock, J. (2001). *Classroom instruction that works: Research-based strategies for increasing student achievement.* Alexandria, VA: Association for Supervision and Curriculum Development.

McKenzie, S. (1995, Spring). Implementing TQM in social studies. *Teaching and Change, 2*(3), 230–244.

Medina, J. (2008). *Brain rules: 12 principles for surviving and thriving at work, home, and school.* Seattle, WA: Pear Press.

Nash, R. (2010). *The active mentor: Practical strategies for supporting new teachers.* Thousand Oaks: Corwin.

Reeves, D. (2009). *Leading change in your school: How to conquer myths, build commitment, and get results.* Alexandria, VA: Association for Supervision and Curriculum Development.

Rooney, J. (2006, September). Unleashing the energy. *Educational Leadership, 64*(1), 91–92.

Schmidt, L. (2002). *Gardening in the minefield: A survival guide for school administrators.* Portsmouth, NH: Heinemann.

Schmoker, M. (1999). *Results: The key to continuous school improvement.* Alexandria, VA: Association for Supervision and Curriculum Development.

Schmoker, M. (2006). *Results now: How we can achieve unprecedented improvements in teaching and learning.* Alexandria, VA: Association for Supervision and Curriculum Development.

Smylie, M. (2010). *Continuous school improvement.* Thousand Oaks, CA: Corwin.

Tapscott, D. (2009). *Grown up digital: How the net generation is changing your world.* New York: McGraw-Hill.

Trilling, B., & Fadel, C. (2009). *21st century skills: Learning for life in our times.* San Francisco: Jossey-Bass.

Vatterott, C. (2009). *Rethinking homework: Best practices that support diverse needs.* Alexandria, VA: Association for Supervision and Curriculum Development.

Wagner, T. (2008). *The global achievement gap: Why even our best schools don't teach the new survival skills our children need—and what we can do about it.* New York: Basic Books.

Wong, H., & Wong, R. (2005). *How to be an effective teacher: The first days of school.* Mountain View, CA: Harry K. Wong Publications.

Index

Note: In page references, f indicates a figure.

CORWIN

A SAGE Company

The Corwin logo—a raven striding across an open book—represents the union of courage and learning. Corwin is committed to improving education for all learners by publishing books and other professional development resources for those serving the field of PreK–12 education. By providing practical, hands-on materials, Corwin continues to carry out the promise of its motto: **"Helping Educators Do Their Work Better."**